CANYONLANDS
NATIONAL PARK
ACTIVITY BOOK

PUZZLES, MAZES, GAMES, AND MORE ABOUT
CANYONLANDS NATIONAL PARK

NATIONAL PARKS ACTIVITIES SERIES

CANYONLANDS NATIONAL PARK ACTIVITY BOOK

LITTLE BISON
Press

For more free national parks activities, visit
www.littlebisonpress.com

About Canyonlands National Park

Canyonlands National Park is located in the state of Utah. Designated as a national park in 1964, Canyonlands is named for its many canyons, as well as other formations such as mesas and buttes.

This park is famous for its dramatic desert landscape. It is also home to the Great Gallery, one of the best examples of rock art in all the US national parks. Horseshoe Canyon's rock markings include pictographs (figures painted on the rock's surface) and petroglyphs (figures etched or carved into the rock). These ancient markings are thought to be from the Late Archaic period and are done in the Barrier Canyon Style. At the time the paintings were made, nomadic groups of hunter-gatherers lived in Horseshoe Canyon seasonally.

Visitors can visit the four different districts in the park: The Needles, The Maze, Horseshoe Canyon, and Island in the Sky. These districts are separated naturally by the Colorado and Green Rivers, but they all share a common environment: the desert. No matter which district you visit, there are lots of opportunities to explore!

Canyonlands National Park is famous for:
- clear night skies for stargazing
- ancient rock art
- red rock canyons

Hey, I'm Parker!

I'm the only snail in history to visit every National Park in the United States! Come join me on my adventures in Canyonlands National Park.

Throughout this book, we will learn about the history of the park, the animals and plants that live here, and things to do if you ever visit in person. This book is also full of games and activities!

Last but not least, I am hidden 9 times on different pages. See how many times you can find me. This page doesn't count!

Canyonlands Bingo

Let's play bingo! Cross off each box you are able to during your visit to the national park. Try to get a bingo down, across, or diagonally. If you can't visit the park, use the bingo board to plan your perfect trip.

Pick out some activities you would want to do during your visit. What would you do first? How long would you spend there? What animals would you try to see?

DRINK EXTRA WATER	SEE HOODOOS	IDENTIFY A TREE	TAKE A PICTURE AT AN OVERLOOK	WATCH A MOVIE AT THE VISITORS CENTER
GO FOR A HIKE	LEARN ABOUT THE INDIGENOUS PEOPLE WHO LIVE IN THIS AREA	WITNESS A SUNRISE OR SUNSET	OBSERVE THE NIGHT SKIES	GO STARGAZING
HEAR A BIRD CALL	SPOT THE COLORADO OR GREEN RIVER	FREE SPACE	SEE THE ROCK ART AT HORSESHOE CANYON	VISIT A RANGER STATION
PICK UP TEN PIECES OF TRASH	GO CAMPING	SEE A KANGAROO RAT	VISIT ISLAND IN THE SKY	SPOT A BIRD OF PREY
VISIT ROADSIDE RUIN	SEE SOMEONE RIDING A HORSE	HAVE A PICNIC	SPOT SOME ANIMAL TRACKS	PARTICIPATE IN A RANGER-LED ACTIVITY

The National Park Logo

The National Park System has over 400 units in the US. Just like Canyonlands National Park, each location is unique or special in some way. The areas include other national parks, historic sites, monuments, seashores, and other recreation areas.

Each element of the National Park emblem represents something that the National Park Service protects. Fill in each blank below to show what each symbol represents.

```
WORD BANK:

MOUNTAINS, ARROWHEAD, BISON,
SEQUOIA TREE, WATER
```

This represents all plants. _____

This represents all animals. _____

This represents the landscapes. _____

This represents the waters protected by the park service. _____

This represents the historical and archeological values. _____

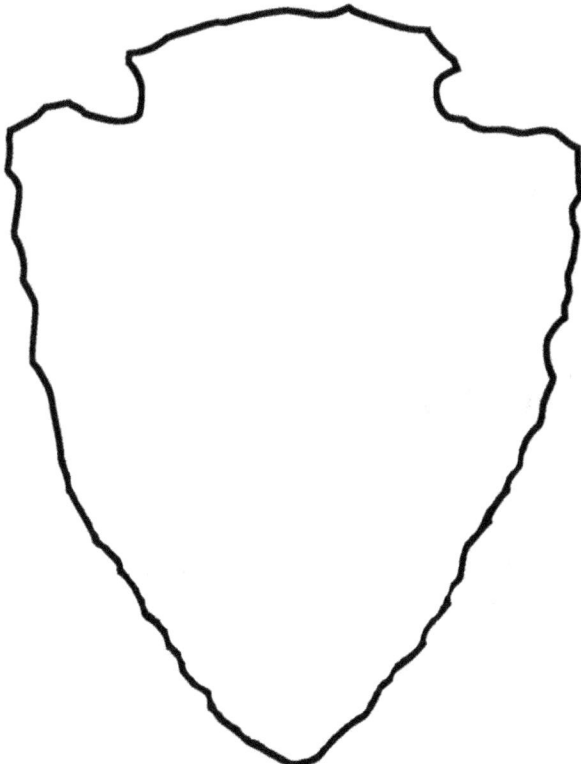

Now it's your turn! Pretend you are designing a new national park. Add elements to the design that represent the things your park protects.

What is the name of your park?

Describe why you included the symbols that you chose. What do they mean?

Things to Do Jumble

Unscramble the letters to uncover activities you can do while in Canyonlands National Park. Hint: each one ends in -ing.

1. KINICPC
⬚⬚⬚⬚⬚⬚⬚ ING

2. KHI
⬚⬚⬚ ING

3. RIBD
⬚⬚⬚⬚ ING

4. MAPC
⬚⬚⬚⬚ ING

5. SARTGZA
⬚⬚⬚⬚⬚⬚⬚ ING

6. ESSTEIGH
⬚⬚⬚⬚⬚⬚⬚⬚ ING

7. RABEHOSRCKID
⬚⬚⬚⬚⬚⬚⬚⬚⬚⬚⬚⬚ ING

Word Bank

birding

reading

camping

stargazing

horseback riding

hiking

skiing

singing

yelling

sightseeing

picnicking

When Nature Calls...

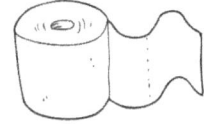

Read the following paragraph to discover the important waste management plays in our national parks. Fill in the blanks with words from the word bank, at right, as you read.

Word Bank:

flush
flow
hard
urinate
ecosystem
pit
never
ashes
plumbing
container
inches
recycling

No matter where you go, don't forget to wash your hands with soap and water afterward! At the very least, pack hand sanitizer to use.

The people who work at national parks are responsible for ensuring proper waste management from guests. Waste management isn't just about making sure trash and _____ go to the right places. It also means human waste! It may not be pleasant to think about, but all humans _____ (pee) and defecate (poop). It is important to consider how to deal with human waste to keep parks clean, safe, and with as little disturbance to the _____ as possible.

There are different types of bathrooms or methods used to deal with human waste. In visitor centers, you are likely to encounter a standard _____ toilet, which uses water and modern _____ to whisk your waste away. Near trails or at campgrounds, you may find toilets that don't flush. A _____ toilet is a type of toilet built over a hole in the ground. A composting toilet decomposes human waste into compost with an aerobic process. A vault toilet stores urine and feces in an underground _____ or vault before it is pumped out. Unlike pit toilets, they are less stinky because of vent pipes, which allow air to _____ from the vault out through the ceiling.

No matter which type of toilet you encounter, there are some things you should keep in mind to help protect the park. First, _____ put anything in the toilet other than pee, poop, or toilet paper. Things like snack wrappers, diapers, or _____ from a campfire can damage toilet systems. It can cost a lot of money and time to fix. Make sure trash goes in the trash can, not any toilet.

If you have to "go" while you are in the backcountry, here is what you should do. If you have to pee, try to urinate on a _____ surface like rocks, not plants. Animals are attracted to the salt in urine and may dig up vegetation to get to it. If you have to poop, you will need to dig a cat hole. First, select a location. It must be at least 200 feet away from any water source. Use a small shovel to dig a hole about 6 _____ deep. Do your business in the hole, then bury ONLY your poop. Take a trash bag with you, as you will need to take your toilet paper with you along with the rest of your trash. If not, animals may dig up the toilet paper which is bad for them.

Camping Packing List

What should you take with you when you go camping? Pretend you are in charge of your family camping trip. Make a list of what you would need to be safe and comfortable on an overnight excursion. Some considerations are listed on the side.

1.

2.

3.

4.

5.

6.

7.

8.

9.

10.

11.

12.

13.

14.

15.

16.

- What will you eat at every meal?

- What will the weather be like?

- Where will you sleep?

- What will you do during your free time?

- How luxurious do you want camp to be?

- How will you cook?

- How will you see at night?

- How will you dispose of trash?

- What might you need in case of emergencies?

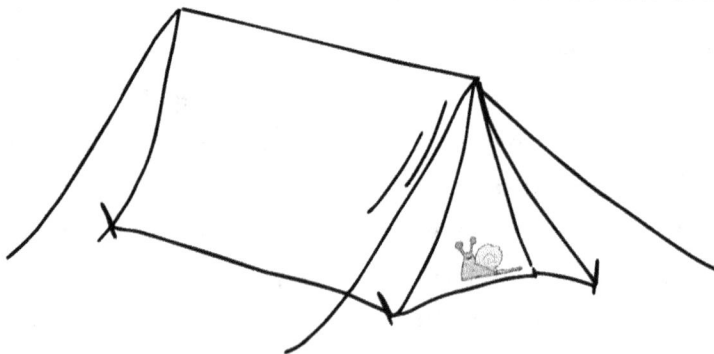

Canyonlands National Park

Date: _____

Season: _____

Who I went with: _____

Which entrance: _____

How was your experience? Write a few sentences about your trip. Where did you stay? What did you do? What was your favorite activity? If you haven't visited the park yet, write a paragraph pretending that you did.

_____

_____

_____

_____

_____

STAMPS

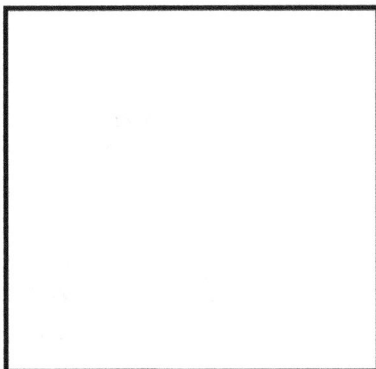

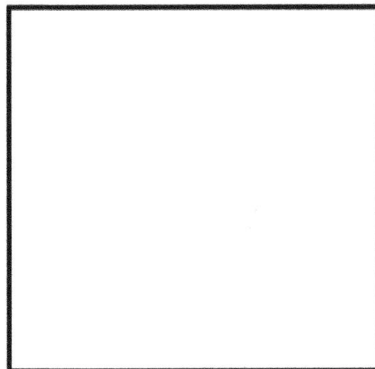

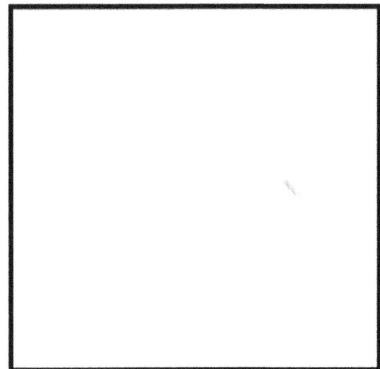

Many national parks and monuments have cancellation stamps for visitors to use. These rubber stamps record the date and location that you visited. Many people collect the markings as a free souvenir. Check with a ranger to see where you can find a stamp during your visit. If you aren't able to find one, you can draw your own.

National Park Names

You may be familiar with places designated as a "national park" but this is just one way parks can be named. There are over 400 units (places) in the National Parks Service (NPS) and quite a few ways these places are titled. Certain qualities of parks are reflected in the variety of titles given to them, and these titles offer clues as to what you might find there. Besides the 63 national parks, there are national monuments, national scenic trails, national battlefields, and many more.

The letters of several designations of NPS units are all jumbled up. Can you unscramble the word and figure out the title?

ERRIV
◯ _ _ R

CETERYME
◯ M _ _ _ _ _

SHSEAREO
S ◯◯ _ _ _ E

ESERVER
◯ S _ _ _ _

ARWAYPK
P _ _ _ ◯ _

MRIAEMOL
◯ _ _ _ A

RELASHOKE
A _ _ _ ◯ R

Now arrange the circled letters to solve one last type of NPS unit.

◯◯◯ R ◯ T I ◯ N A R ◯◯

Where is the Park?

Canyonlands National Park is in the western United States. It is located in Utah. The nickname for Utah is the Beehive State. Can you find Utah on the map?

Utah

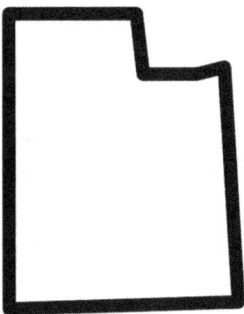

Look at the shape of Utah. Can you find it on the map? If you are from the US, can you find your home state? Color Utah red. Put a star on the map where you live.

Go Birdwatching at Island in the Sky

start here

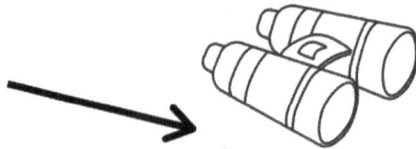

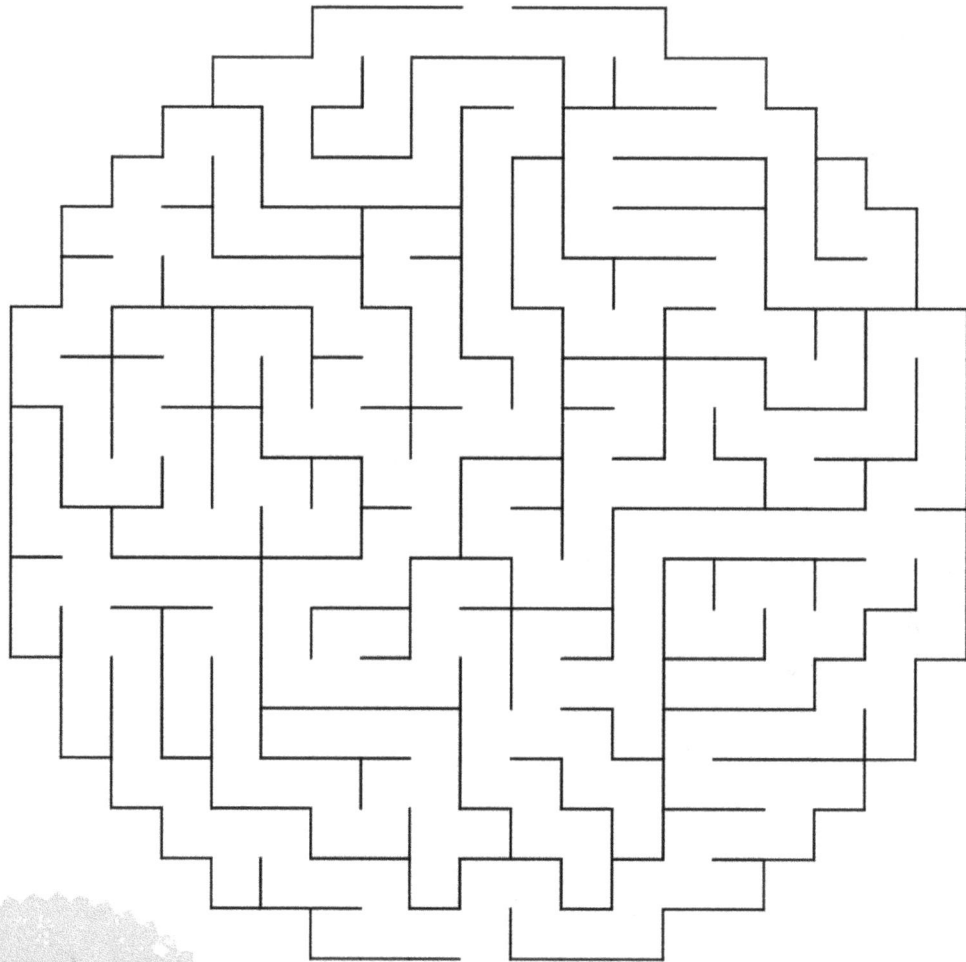

DID YOU KNOW?
Canyonlands National Park is home to several birds of prey, including eagles, hawks, and owls. Birds of prey are birds that hunt other animals for food.

Animals of Canyonlands National Park

Badgers are a member of the weasel family. They use their huge front claws to dig their burrows.

Woodhouse's Toads are a gray-green color with dark spots.

Striped Skunks are known for their stinky defense mechanism.

Greater Short-horned Lizards can squirt blood from their eyes to deter predators from eating them.

Peregrine Falcons are known for their speed and agility, diving through the air at over 200 miles per hour to catch their prey.

Design a Sweatshirt

Imagine you are a graphic designer and you have been hired to design a sweatshirt that will be for sale in the Island in the Sky Visitor Center. Use your knowledge of Canyonlands National Park to create a meaningful souvenir.

Your design should include:

- the name of the park
- the year the park was established
- 2 or more colors that represent the park
- 1 symbol or feature of the park

Use colored pencils, crayons, or markers to make your designs. You can include artwork on the sleeves too!

Draw a Bear

Complete the picture below by drawing the other half of the bear. Complete the image by coloring it in.

There are black bears that live in the nearby Abajo Mountains. They aren't commonly seen in the park, but it is important for campers and backpackers to be careful with their food to avoid attracting bears.

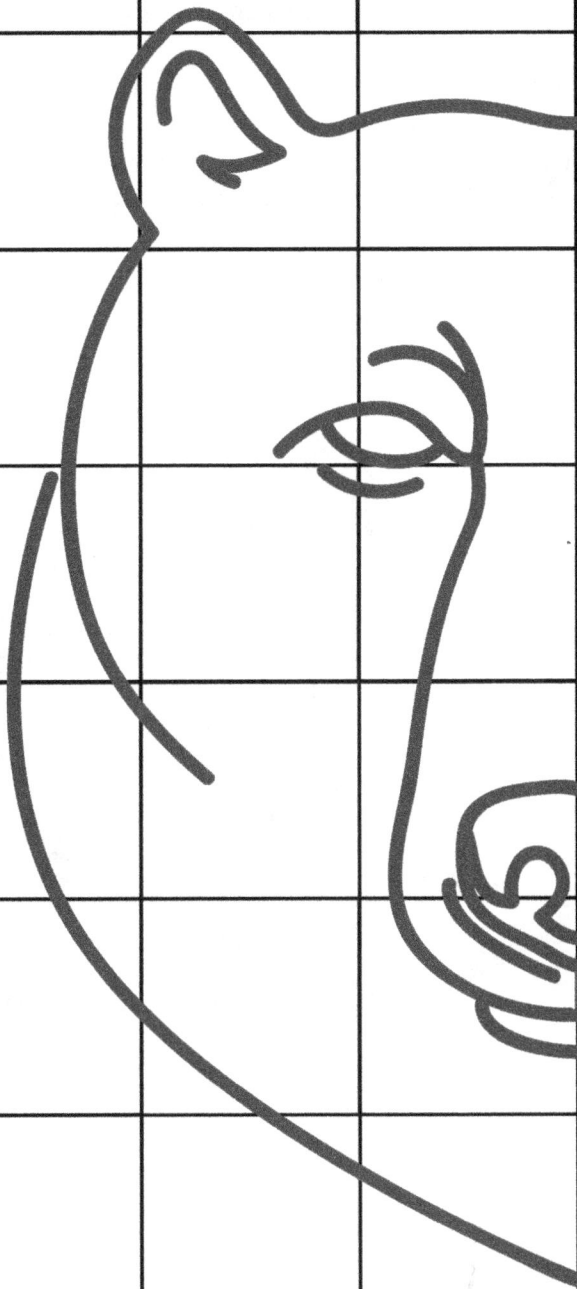

Common Names
vs.
Scientific Names

A common name of an organism is a name that is based on everyday language. You have heard the common names of plants, animals, and other living things on tv, in books, and at school. Common names can also be referred to as "English" names, popular names, or farmer's names. Common names can vary from place to place. The word for a particular tree may be one thing, but that same tree has a different name in another country. Common names can even vary from region to region, even in the same country.

Scientific names, or Latin names, are given to organisms to make it possible to have uniform names for the same species. Scientific names are in Latin. You may have heard plants or animals referred to by their scientific name or parts of their scientific names. Latin names are also called "binomial nomenclature," which refers to a two-part naming system. The first part of the name - the generic name - refers to the genus to which the species belongs. The second part of the name, the specific name, identifies the species. For example, Tyrannosaurus rex is an example of a widely known scientific name.

American Black Bear

Ursus americanus

COMMON NAME

Bighorn Sheep

Ovis canadensis

LATIN NAME = GENUS + SPECIES

Bighorn Sheep = Ovis canadensis

Black Bear = Ursus americanus

Find the Match!
Common Names and Latin Names

Match the common name to the scientific name for each animal. The first one is done for you. Use clues on the page before and after this one to complete the matches.

Bighorn Sheep   Haliaeetus leucocephalus

Two-needle Piñon   Ursus americanus

Cheatgrass   Pandion haliaetus

American Black Bear   Opuntia engelmannii

Great Horned Owl   Pinus edulis

Bald Eagle   Aspidoscelis uniparens

Osprey   Bubo virginianus

Prickly Pear   Ovis canadensis

Whiptail   Bromus tectorum

Bald Eagle

Haliaeetus leucocephalus

Osprey
Pandion haliaetus

Two-needle Piñon
Pinus edulis

Great Horned Owl
Bubo virginianus

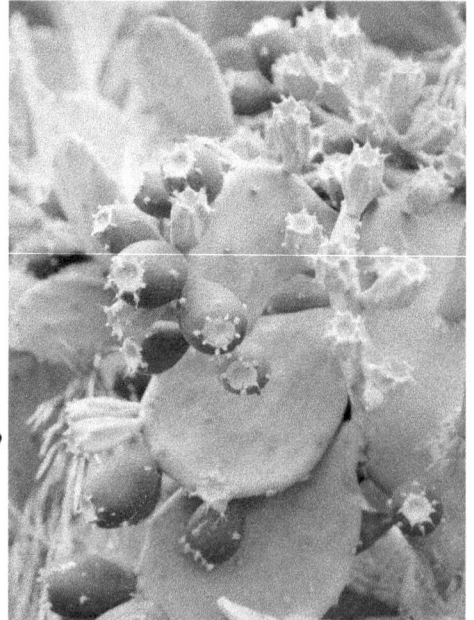

Some plants and animals that live in Utah

Prickly Pear
Opuntia engelmannii

Cheatgrass
Bromus tectorum

Whiptail
Aspidoscelis uniparens

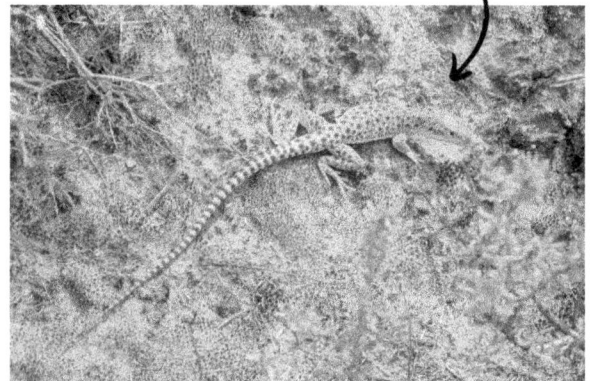

Photobook

Draw some pictures of
things you saw in the park.

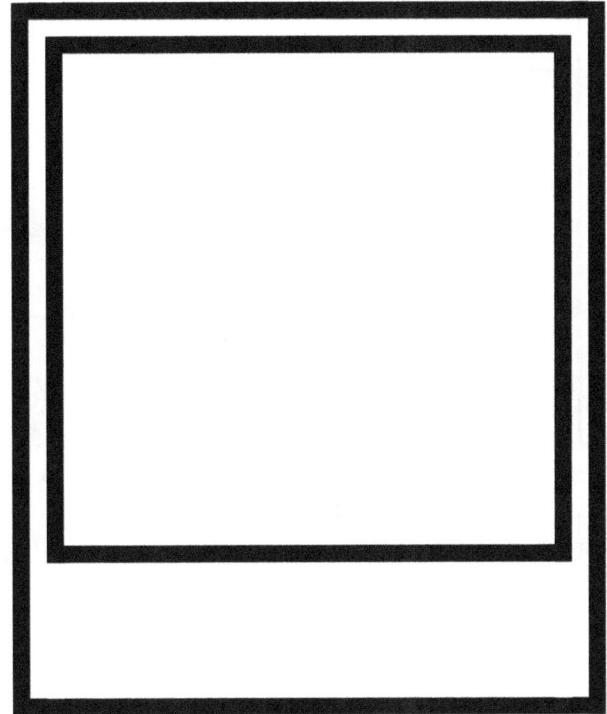

The Ten Essentials

The ten essentials are a list of things that are important to have when you go for longer hikes. If you go on a hike to the <u>backcountry</u>, it is especially important that you have everything you need in case of an emergency. If you get lost or something unforeseen happens, it is good to be prepared to survive until help finds you.

The ten essentials list was developed in the 1930s by an outdoors group called the Mountaineers. Over time and technological advancements, this list has evolved. Can you identify all the things on the current list? Circle each of the "essentials" and cross out everything that doesn't make the cut.

fire: matches, lighter, tinder, and/or stove	a pint of milk	extra money	headlamp, plus extra batteries	extra clothes
extra water	a dog	Polaroid camera	bug net	lightweight games, such as a deck of cards
extra food	a roll of duct tape	shelter	sun protection such as sunglasses, sun-protective clothes, and sunscreen	knife, plus a gear repair kit
a mirror	navigation: map, compass, altimeter, GPS device, or satellite messenger	first aid kit	extra flip-flops	entertainment such as video games or books

Backcountry - a remote undeveloped rural area.

Staying Safe in the Sun

It is important to take precautions to stay safe outdoors, especially when it is very hot outside. When someone gets overheated or dehydrated, they may feel sick or even require medical attention.

Use the cryptogram below to decode three tips on how to prevent heat-related illnesses. You may need to do some math to figure out the answers.

T _ _ _   _ _ _ _ _ _   _ _   _ _ _ _
12 5 12/2 50   30 21 50 5 2x3 36   3x4 27   21 50 6x6 12

_ _   _ _ _   _ _ _ _ _ .
99 10   15-3 4 50   36 7-3 5 1 50

_ _ _ _   H _ _ _ _ _ _ _   _ _
36 12 1x5 18   4 2x9 1 21 5 12 50 8-7   30 18

_ _ _ _ _ _ _ _ _   _ _ _ _   _ _   _ _ _ _ _ .
1 21 99 10 6 33x3 10 75   35 3x9 12 36   27 5x5   18/2 5 12 50 21

_ _ A _   _ _ _ _ _ _ _ _ _ _   _ _ _
9 50 12-7 21   36 3 10 36 15 21 5x10 50 10   5 10 12-11

_ _ _   - _ _ _ _ _ _ _ _ _
36 3 10   8 7x3 27 12 50 15 9+3 99 80 50

_ _ _ _ _ I N G .
15 35 27 12 2x2 99 10 75

a	b	c	d	e	f	g	h	i	j	k	l	m	n	o
5	30	15	1	50	25	75	4	99	20	6	35	49	10	27

p	q	r	s	t	u	v	w	x	y	z
8	16	21	36	12	3	80	9	40	18	7

Making a Difference

It is important to protect the valuable resources of the world, not only beautiful places like national parks.

How many of these things do you do at home? If you answered "no" to more than 10 items, talk to the grown-ups in your life to see if there are any household habits you might be able to change. Conserving our collective resources helps us all.

Yes	No	Do you...
☐	☐	turn off the water when brushing your teeth?
☐	☐	use LED light bulbs when possible?
☐	☐	use a reusable water bottle instead of disposable ones?
☐	☐	ride your bike or take the bus instead of riding in the car?
☐	☐	have a rain barrel under your roof gutters to collect rain water?
☐	☐	take quick showers?
☐	☐	avoid putting more food on your plate than you will eat?
☐	☐	take reusable lunch containers?
☐	☐	grow a garden?
☐	☐	buy items with less packaging?
☐	☐	recycle paper?
☐	☐	recycle plastic?
☐	☐	have a compost pile at home so you can make your own soil?
☐	☐	pick up trash when you see it on the trail?
☐	☐	plan a "staycation" and fly only when you have to?

_____   _____

\# of Yes   \# of No

Add up your score! Are there any "no"s that you want to turn into a yes?

Can you think of any other ways to protect our natural resources?

_____

LISTEN CAREFULLY

Visitors to Canyonlands National Park may hear different noises from those they hear at home. Try this activity to experience this for yourself!

First, find a place outside where it is comfortable to sit or stand for a few minutes. You can do this by yourself or with a friend or family member. Once you have a good spot, close your eyes and listen. Be quiet for one minute and pay attention to what you are hearing. List some of the sounds you have heard in one of the two boxes below:

NATURAL SOUNDS
MADE BY ANIMALS, TREES OR PLANTS, THE WIND, ETC

HUMAN-MADE SOUNDS
MADE BY PEOPLE, MACHINES, ETC

ONCE YOU ARE BACK AT HOME, TRY REPEATING YOUR EXPERIMENT:

NATURAL SOUNDS
MADE BY ANIMALS, TREES OR PLANTS, THE WIND, ETC

HUMAN-MADE SOUNDS
MADE BY PEOPLE, MACHINES, ETC

WHERE DID YOU HEAR MORE NATURAL SOUNDS? _____

WHERE DID YOU HEAR MORE HUMAN SOUNDS? _____

Snail Mail

Design a postcard to send to a friend or family member. Who do you want to tell about Canyonlands National Park? In the first template, write your message. In the second template, create a design for the front of the postcard. You could show something you saw, something you did, or something you want to do in the national park.

Postcard

_____

_____

_____

_____

Canyonlands Word Search

Words may be horizontal, vertical, diagonal,
or they might even be backwards!

1. NEEDLES
2. VULTURES
3. HIGH DESERT
4. SKY
5. MAZE
6. GREEN RIVER
7. MOAB
8. MAZE TRAILS
9. BOATING
10. CAIRN
11. SPIRE
12. MESA
13. WEATHER
14. NARROWLEAF
15. PINYON
16. BIGHORN
17. STARGAZING

```
M O A B G N I M N R I A C D M
E A I E P W A N R A O R U T H
O L Z M A I T H O U R I N G O
S N E E D L E S H Y V R T H A
T D E S T Y O T G S N P O G H
A G D A L R G H I I S I N W I
R E G N I T A O B G V A P N G
G L M A R Y O I E U E T I R H
A T N A R R O W L E A F W C D
Z S Y U H E S T T S N A S A E
I G R A F E U D R C A N T M S
N N D H R R R G R K H M A Z E
G I E W E A I O I F T I P I R
D P B S R S N N N A S K Y N T
R M N L E R G D S C P N U G O
W E A T H E R E L E I A M E N
O C R T R A V E R T R N E W D
B O G R E E N R I V E R A D M
```

Find the Match!
What are Baby Animals Called?

Match the animal to its baby. The first one is done for you.

Elk	eaglet
Bald Eagle	calf
Little Brown Bat	snakelets
Striped Skunk	pup
Great Horned Owl	owlet
Western Toad	kit
Mountain Lion	tadpole
Garter snake	kitten

Reducing Your Footprint

Your carbon "footprint" is the amount of carbon dioxide released into the air because of your own energy needs. All people have basic needs like transportation, electricity, food, clothing, and other goods. Governments and private businesses have the biggest impact on the environment, but our individual choices can impact the planet too.

In the box below, make a footprint. You can use your own foot and trace it, step in paint and make a footprint, or draw a footprint freehand.

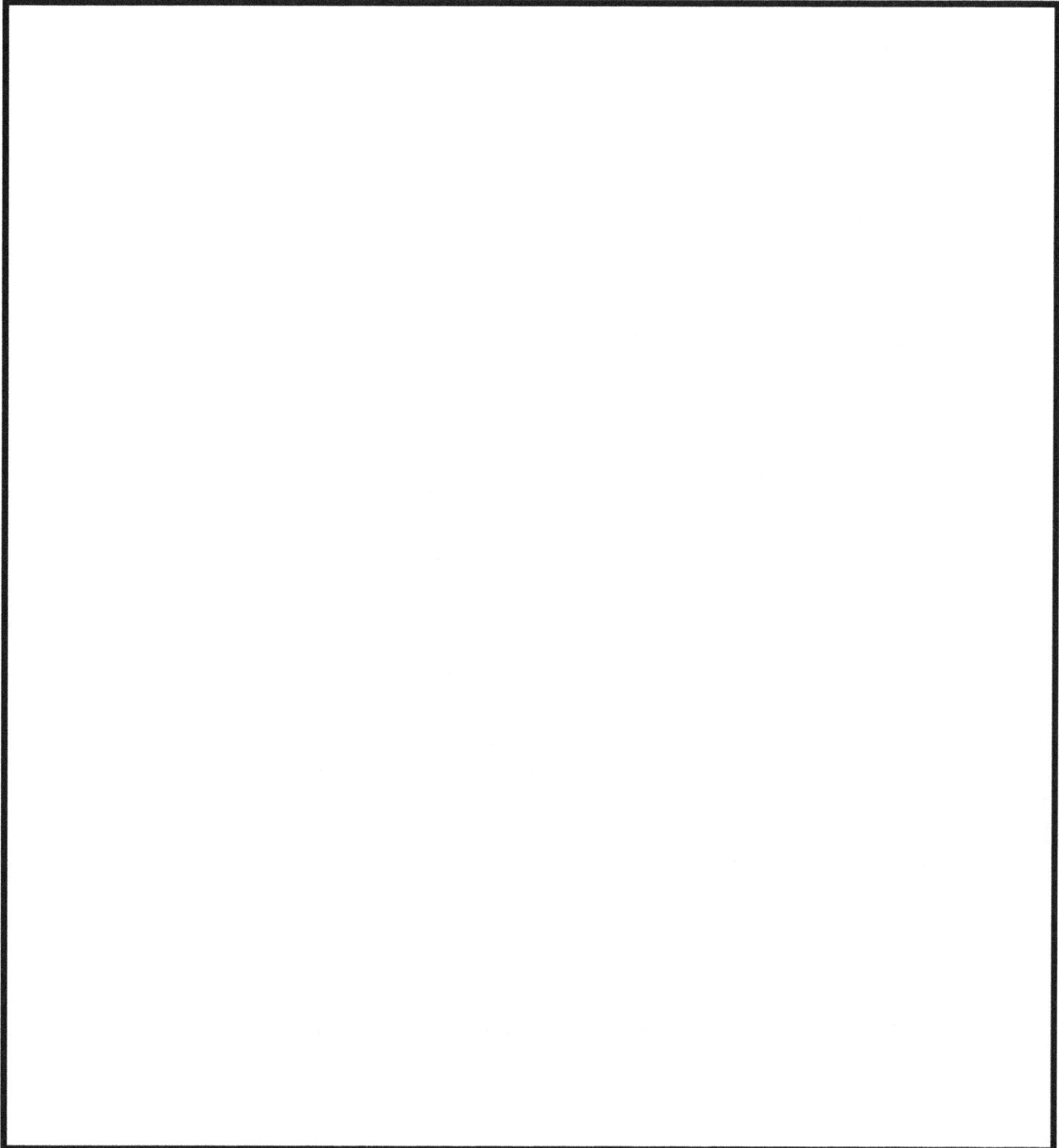

How does your community try to reduce its carbon footprint? You can use examples from your town, your school, or your family. See page 22 for ideas.

The Perfect Picnic Spot

Fill in the blanks on this page without looking at the full story. Once you have each line filled out, use the words you've chosen to complete the story on the next page.

EMOTION _____

FOOD _____

SOMETHING SWEET _____

STORE _____

MODE OF TRANSPORTATION _____

NOUN _____

SOMETHING ALIVE _____

SAUCE _____

PLURAL VEGETABLES _____

ADJECTIVE _____

PLURAL BODY PART _____

ANIMAL _____

PLURAL FRUIT _____

PLACE _____

SOMETHING TALL _____

COLOR _____

ADJECTIVE _____

NOUN _____

A DIFFERENT ANIMAL _____

FAMILY MEMBER #1 _____

FAMILY MEMBER #2 _____

VERB THAT ENDS IN -ING _____

A DIFFERENT FOOD _____

The Perfect Picnic Spot

Use the words from the previous page to complete a silly story.

When my family suggested having our lunch at the Island in the Sky picnic area,

I was _____. I love eating my _____ outside! I knew we had picked up a
　　　　EMOTION　　　　　　　　　　　　　　FOOD

box of _____ from the _____ for after lunch, my favorite. We drove up
　　　SOMETHING SWEET　　　STORE

to the area and I jumped out of the _____. "I will find the perfect spot for
　　　　　　　　　　　　　　　　　MODE OF TRANSPORTATION

a picnic!" I grabbed a _____ for us to sit on, and I ran off. I passed a picnic
　　　　　　　　　　NOUN

table, but it was covered with _____ so we couldn't sit there. The next picnic
　　　　　　　　　　　SOMETHING ALIVE

table looked okay, but there were smears of _____ and pieces of _____
　　　　　　　　　　　　　　　　　　　　　SAUCE　　　　　　　PLURAL VEGETABLES

everywhere. The people that were there before must have been _____! I
　　　　　　　　　　　　　　　　　　　　　　　　　　　　ADJECTIVE

gritted my _____ together and kept walking down the path, determined to
　　　　　PLURAL BODY PART

find the perfect spot. I wanted a table with a good view of the canyon. Why was

this so hard? If we were lucky, I might even get to see _____ eating some
　　　　　　　　　　　　　　　　　　　　　　　　　　ANIMAL

_____ on the cliffside. They don't have those in _____ where I am from. I
PLURAL FRUIT　　　　　　　　　　　　　　　　PLACE

walked down a little hill and there it was, the perfect spot! The trees towered

overhead and looked as tall as _____. The patch of grass was a beautiful
　　　　　　　　　　　　　SOMETHING TALL

_____ color. The _____ flowers were growing on
COLOR　　　　　　ADJECTIVE

the side of a _____. I looked across the canyon edge and even saw a
　　　　　NOUN

_____ on the edge of a rock. I looked back to see my _____ and
DIFFERENT ANIMAL　　　　　　　　　　　　　　　　　　　FAMILY MEMBER #1

_____ _____ a picnic basket. "I hope you brought plenty of
FAMILY MEMBER #2　VERB THAT ENDS IN ING

_____, I'm starving!"
A DIFFERENT FOOD

29

Hike to a Hoodoo

start here

DID YOU KNOW?
Hoodoos are tall, thin rocks that protrude from the bottom of a basin. Have you seen any in the park?

Utah Word Search

Words may be horizontal, vertical, diagonal,
or they might be backwards!

1. OSPREY
2. UTAH
3. SOUTHWEST
4. CANYON
5. EXPLORE
6. REPTILE
7. DRY
8. DESERT
9. HIKING
10. ROCKS
11. SALT LAKE CITY
12. GEOLOGY
13. PINYON PINE
14. PINE NUTS
15. CLIFFS
16. BEEHIVE
17. ARID
18. CACTUS

```
C W S O U T H W E S T L O W K
H T A A K I L O C H E L A N J
T G E O L O G Y C C L B A P E
P M P A Y T R S C E R L H L X
I I A D R A L L O E I U I A P
N O N D D I R A D C T T K S L
Y E S E E H E K K B P R I C O
O L B A N U I E G E N E N A R
N E H S G U L O R E C D G D E
P C I C A C T U S H P I O E A
I T A L C H I S O I K E T S N
N R N I K O E I O V O K I Y E
E I O F H Z D E S E R T L G W
J C G F L O V E P O O R V E H
N I L S K H I N R O C K S E A
X T A I A E E G E Z E P R N L
H T D T O E N O Y N A C C I E
U J U O S N E D N Y M A L A Z
```

31

Leave No Trace Quiz

Leave No Trace is a concept that helps people make decisions during outdoor recreation that protects the environment. There are seven principles that guide us when we spend time outdoors, whether you are in a national park or not. Are you an expert in Leave No Trace? Take this quiz and find out!

1. How can you plan ahead and prepare to ensure you have the best experience you can in the national park?
   a. Make sure you stop by the ranger station for a map and to ask about current conditions.
   b. Just wing it! You will know the best trail when you see it.
   c. Stick to your plan, even if conditions change. You traveled a long way to get here, and you should stick to your plan.

2. What is an example of traveling on a durable surface?
   a. Walking only on the designated path.
   b. Walking on the grass that borders the trail if the trail is very muddy.
   c. Taking a shortcut if you can find one because it means you will be walking less.

3. Why should you dispose of waste properly?
   a. You don't need to. Park rangers love to pick up the trash you leave behind.
   b. You should actually leave your leftovers behind, because animals will eat them. It is important to make sure they aren't hungry.
   c. So that other peoples' experiences of the park are not impacted by you leaving your waste behind.

4. How can you best follow the concept "leave what you find?"
   a. Take only a small rock or leaf to remember your trip.
   b. Take pictures, but leave any physical items where they are.
   c. Leave everything you find, unless it may be rare like an arrowhead, then it is okay to take.

5. What is not a good example of minimizing campfire impacts?
   a. Only having a campfire in a pre-existing campfire ring.
   b. Checking in with current conditions when you consider making a campfire.
   c. Building a new campfire ring in a location that has a better view.

6. What is a poor example of respecting wildlife?
   a. Building squirrel houses out of rocks so the squirrels have a place to live.
   b. Stay far away from wildlife and give them plenty of space.
   c. Reminding your grown-ups not to drive too fast in animal habitats while visiting the park.

7. How can you show consideration of other visitors?
   a. Play music on your speaker so other people at the campground can enjoy it.
   b. Wear headphones on the trail if you choose to listen to music.
   c. Make sure to yell "Hello!" to every animal you see at top volume.

Park Poetry

America's parks inspire art of all kinds. Painters, sculptors, photographers, writers, and artists of all mediums have taken inspiration from natural beauty. They have turned their inspiration into great works.

Use this space to write your own poem about the park. Think about what you have experienced or seen. Use descriptive language to create an acrostic poem. This type of poem has the first letter of each line spell out another word. Create an acrostic that spells out the word "Utah."

U _____

T _____

A _____

H _____

Under big sky

Towering rocks

All around me

Hot dry land

Up in the air

Top predator

A bird so ferocious

Hovering over its prey

Bird Scavenger Hunt

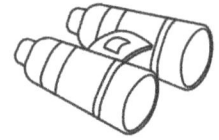

Canyonlands National Park is a great place to go birdwatching. You don't have to be able to identify different species of birds in order to have fun. Open your eyes and tune in your ears. Check off as many birds on this list as you can.

☐ A colorful bird   ☐ A big bird

☐ A brown bird   ☐ A small bird

☐ A bird in a tree   ☐ A hopping bird

☐ A bird with long tail feathers   ☐ A flying bird

☐ A bird making noise   ☐ A bird's nest

☐ A bird eating or hunting   ☐ A bird's footprint on the ground

☐ A bird with spots   ☐ A bird with stripes somewhere on it

What was the easiest bird on the list to find? What was the hardest?
Why do you think that was?

_____

_____

_____

Catch a Fish in the Colorado River

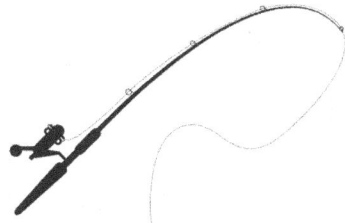

start here

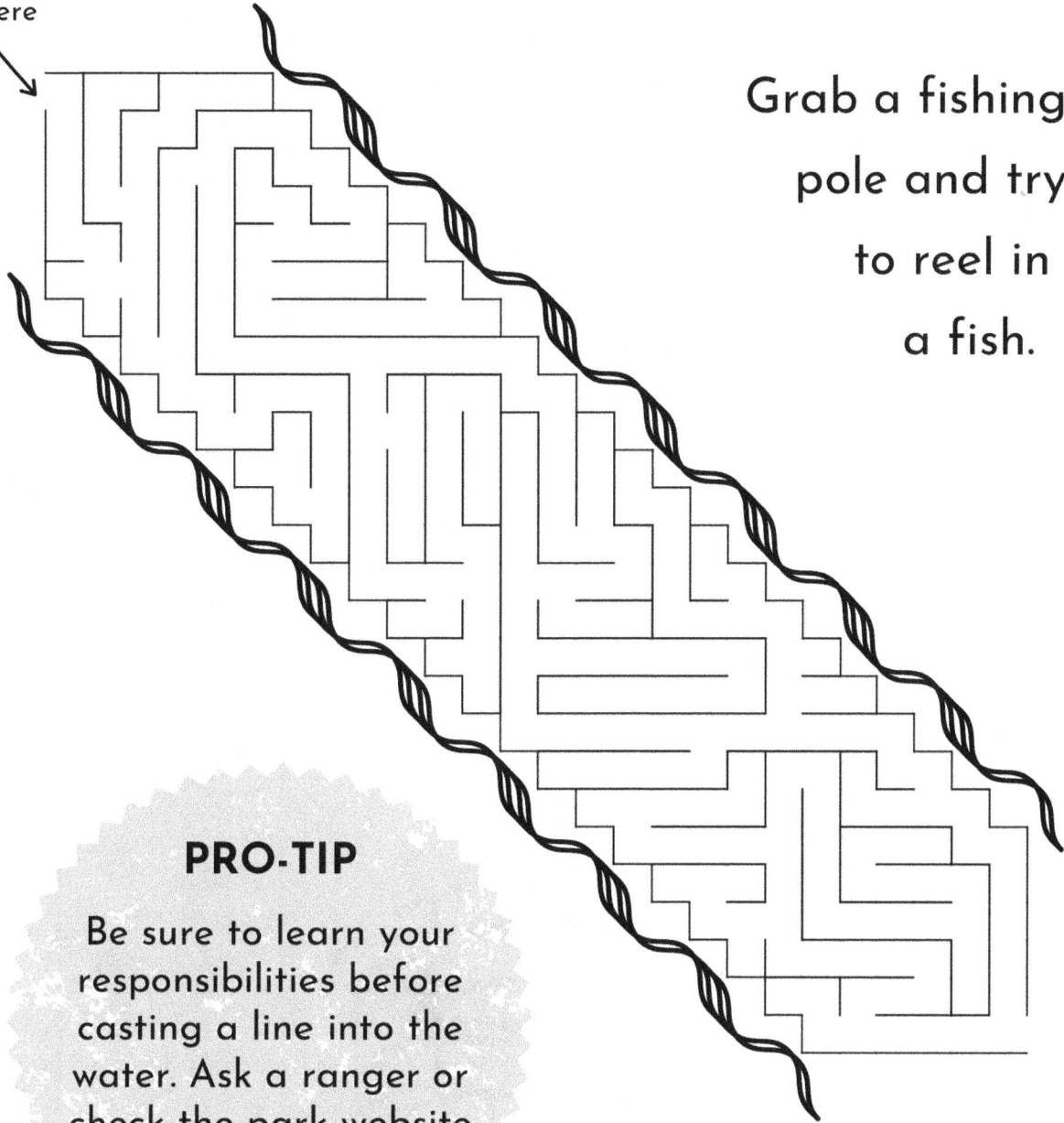

Grab a fishing pole and try to reel in a fish.

PRO-TIP

Be sure to learn your responsibilities before casting a line into the water. Ask a ranger or check the park website before you go.

Stacking Rocks

Have you ever seen stacks of rocks while hiking in national parks? Do you know what they are or what they mean? These rock piles are called cairns and often mark hiking routes in parks. Every park has a different way to maintain trails and cairns. However, they all have the same rule: If you come across a cairn, do not disturb it!

Color the cairn and the rules to remember.

1. Do not tamper with cairns.

If a cairn is tampered with or an unauthorized one is built, then future visitors may become disoriented or even lost.

2. Do not build unauthorized cairns.

Moving rocks disturbs the soil and makes the area more prone to erosion. Disturbing rocks can disturb fragile plants.

3. Do not add to existing cairns.

Authorized cairns are carefully designed. Adding to them can actually cause them to collapse.

Decoding Using American Sign Language

American Sign Language, also called ASL for short, is a language that many Deaf people or people who are hard of hearing use to communicate. People use ASL to communicate with their hands. Did you know people from all over the country and world travel to national parks? You may hear people speaking other languages. You might also see people using ASL. Use the American Manual Alphabet chart to decode some national parks facts.

This was the first national park to be established:

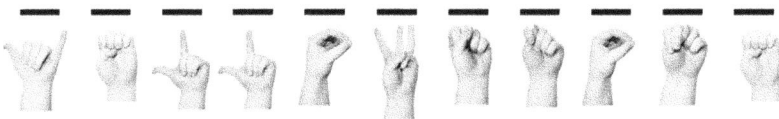

_ _ _ _ _ _ _ _ _ _

This is the biggest national park in the US:

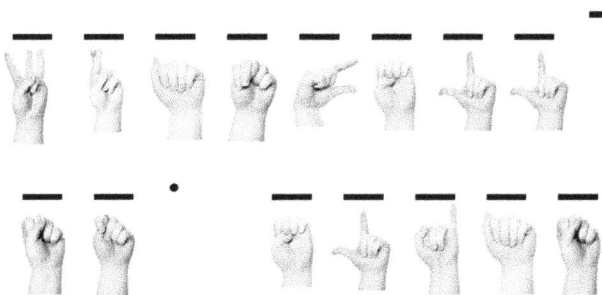

_ _ _ _ _ _ _ _ -

_ _ . _ _ _ _

This is the most visited national park:

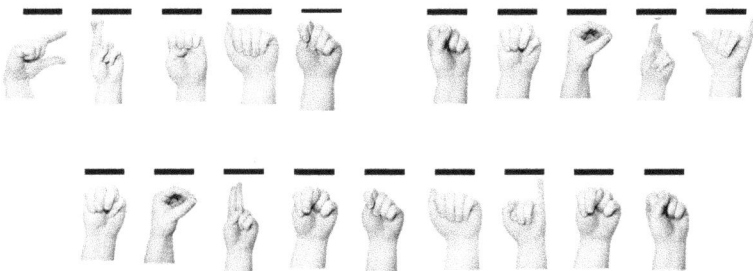

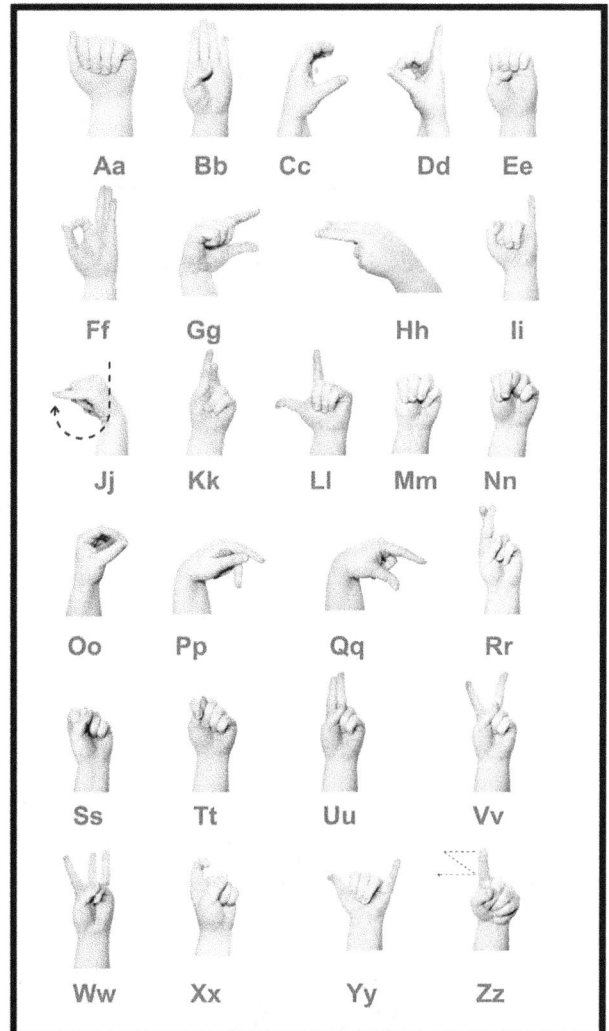

_ _ _ _ _ _ _ _ _

_ _ _ _ _ _ _

Aa	Bb	Cc	Dd	Ee
Ff	Gg		Hh	Ii
Jj	Kk	Ll	Mm	Nn
Oo	Pp	Qq		Rr
Ss	Tt	Uu		Vv
Ww	Xx	Yy		Zz

Hint: Pay close attention to the position of the thumb!

Try it! Using the chart, try to make the letters of the alphabet with your hand. What is the hardest letter to make? Can you spell out your name? Show a friend or family member and have them watch you spell out the name of the national park you are in.

Go Horseback Riding at
Horseshoe Canyon

Help find the horse's lost shoe!

start
here

DID YOU KNOW?

Horseback riding is a popular activity in Canyonlands National Park. There are many trails that you can take horses for day or overnight trips.

Butterflies of the Utah Desert

Dozens of species of butterflies and moths live in Canyonlands National Park. Their wingspan size varies, as do the patterns on their wings. Design your own butterfly below. Make sure the wings are symmetrical, which means both sides match.

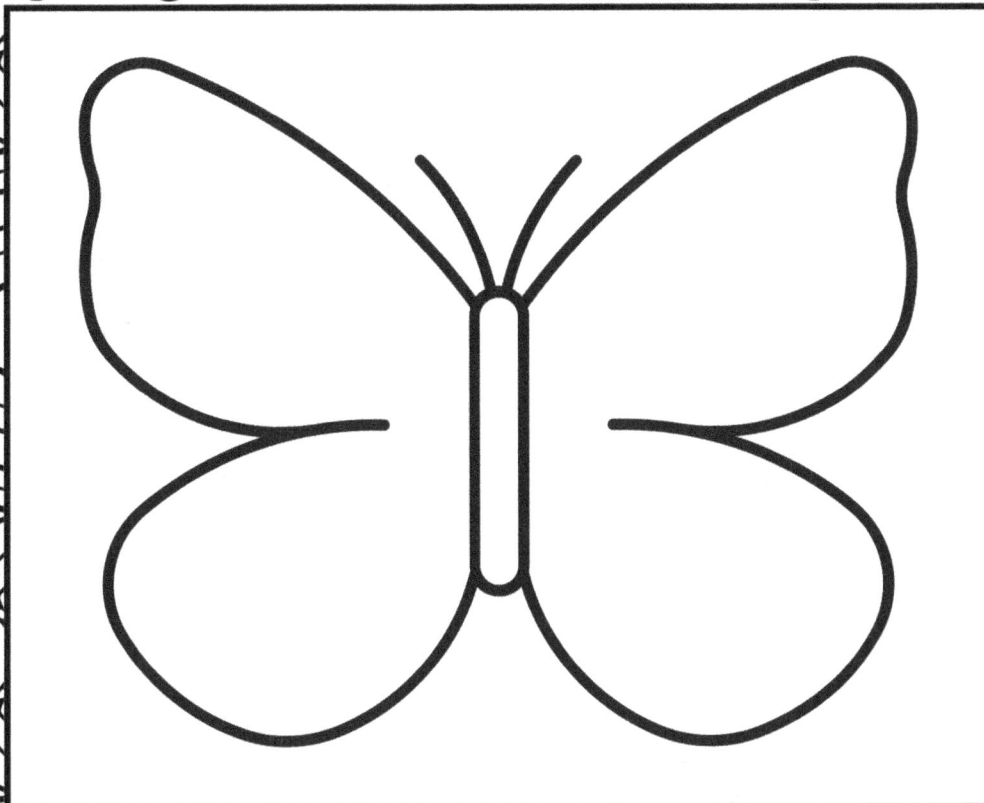

A Hike at Grand View Point

Fill in the blanks on this page without looking at the full story. Once you have each line filled out, use the words you've chosen to complete the story on the next page.

ADJECTIVE _____

SOMETHING TO EAT _____

SOMETHING TO DRINK _____

NOUN _____

ARTICLE OF CLOTHING _____

BODY PART _____

VERB _____

ANIMAL _____

SAME TYPE OF FOOD _____

ADJECTIVE _____

SAME ANIMAL _____

VERB THAT ENDS IN "ED" _____

NUMBER _____

A DIFFERENT NUMBER _____

SOMETHING THAT FLIES _____

LIGHT SOURCE _____

PLURAL NOUN _____

FAMILY MEMBER _____

YOUR NICKNAME _____

A Hike at Grand View Point

Use the words from the previous page to complete a silly story.

I went for a hike at Grand View Point today. In my favorite _ _ _ _ _ _ _
ADJECTIVE

backpack, I made sure to pack a map so I wouldn't get lost. I also threw in an

extra _ _ _ _ _ _ _ _ _ _ just in case I got hungry and a bottle of _ _ _ _ _ _ _ _ _ _.
SOMETHING TO EAT   SOMETHING TO DRINK

I put on my _ _ _ _ _ _ _ _ _ spray, and I tied a _ _ _ _ _ _ _ _ _ _ _ _ around my
NOUN   ARTICLE OF CLOTHING

_ _ _ _ _ _ _ _ _ _, in case it gets chilly. I started to _ _ _ _ _ _ down the path. As
BODY PART   VERB

soon as I turned the corner, I came face to face with a(n) _ _ _ _ _ _ _ _. I think
ANIMAL

it was as startled as I was! What should I do? I had to think fast! Should I

give it some of my _ _ _ _ _ _ _ _ _ _? No. I had to remember what the
SAME TYPE OF FOOD

_ _ _ _ _ _ _ ranger told me: "If you see one, back away slowly and try not to
ADJECTIVE

scare it." Soon enough, the _ _ _ _ _ _ _ _ _ _ _ _ _ _ _ _ _ _ _ away. The coast
SAME ANIMAL   VERB THAT ENDS IN ED

was clear. _ _ _ _ _ _ hours later, I finally got to the lookout. I felt like I could
NUMBER

see for a _ _ _ _ _ _ miles. I took a picture of a _ _ _ _ _ _ _ _ so I could always
A DIFFERENT NUMBER   NOUN

remember this moment. As I was putting my camera away, a _ _ _ _ _ _ _ _ _
SOMETHING THAT FLIES

flew by, reminding me that it was almost nighttime. I turned on my

_ _ _ _ _ _ _ _ _ _ and headed back. I could hear the _ _ _ _ _ _ _ _ _ _ singing their
LIGHT SOURCE   PLURAL INSECT

evening song. Just as I was getting tired, I saw my _ _ _ _ _ _ _ _ _ _ and our tent.
FAMILY MEMBER

"Welcome back _ _ _ _ _ _ _ _! How was your hike?"
NICKNAME

The Dazzling Desert

People come from all over the world to experience the wonders of the desert at Canyonlands National Park. If you are able to see the desert for yourself, make some observations. Draw or describe them in the boxes below, using lots of detail.

Something colorful	A desert rock	Something that moves
An insect	Something cool you saw	A tiny plant
Something with a smell	A leaf	Something shiny

Let's Go Camping
Word Search

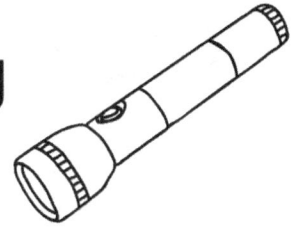

Words may be horizontal, vertical, diagonal, or they might even be backwards!

1. TENT
2. CAMP STOVE
3. SLEEPING BAG
4. BUG SPRAY
5. SUNSCREEN
6. MAP
7. FLASHLIGHT
8. PILLOW
9. LANTERN
10. ICE
11. SNACKS
12. SMORES
13. WATER
14. FIRST AID KIT
15. CHAIR
16. CARDS
17. BOOKS
18. GAMES
19. TRAIL
20. HAT

```
D P P I L L O W D B T E A C I
E O A D P R E A A M B R C A N
P W C A M P S T O V E I H X G
R A H S G E L E B E E D A P S
E L B U G S P R A Y N G I E A
S I A H G C I C N N M E R C N
C W N L A F I R S K O O B F K
M T A E M I L E L H M R W L J
T A P R E A O R E S L B A A B
S M P A S R R T E N T L U S C
C E A I I R C G P E I U J H A
S S N A C K S S I M O K I L R
I J R S F O I S N J R A Q I D
C Y E T L E V E G U O R V G S
E W T A K C A B B S S O H H M
X J N F I R S T A I D K I T T
U A A E S S E N G E T P V A B
C J L I A R T D N A M A H A S
```

All in the Day of a Park Ranger

Park Rangers are hardworking individuals dedicated to protecting our parks, monuments, museums, and more. They take care of the natural and cultural resources for future generations. Rangers also help protect the visitors of the park. Their responsibilities are broad and they work both with the public and behind the scenes.

What have you seen park rangers do? Use your knowledge of the duties of park rangers to fill out a typical daily schedule, listing one activity for each hour. Feel free to make up your own, but some examples of activities are provided on the right. Read carefully! Not all the example activities are befitting a ranger.

Time	Activity		Examples
6 am	Lead a sunrise hike		• feed the bald eagles
7 am			• build trails for visitors to enjoy
8 am			• throw rocks off the side of the mountain
9 am			• rescue lost hikers
10 am			• study animal behavior
11 am			• record air quality data
12 pm	Enjoy a lunch break outside		• answer questions at the visitor center
1 pm			• pick wildflowers
2 pm			• pick up litter
3 pm			• share marshmallows with squirrels
4 pm	Teach visitors about the geology of the area		• repair handrails
5 pm			• lead a class on a field trip
6 pm			• catch toads and make them race
7 pm			• lead people on educational hikes
8 pm			• write articles for the park website
9 pm			• protect the river from pollution

Additional examples:
- remove non-native plants from the park
- study how climate change is affecting the park
- give a talk about geology
- lead a program for campers on bighorn sheep

If you were a park ranger, which of the above tasks would you enjoy most?

_____

_____

44

Draw Yourself as a Park Ranger

RANGER

Fish at Canyonlands National Park

1. FITSCAH

2. OTRTU

Unscramble the common names of these fish that live in the park.

3. LASNOM

4. SISHFUN

5. SABS

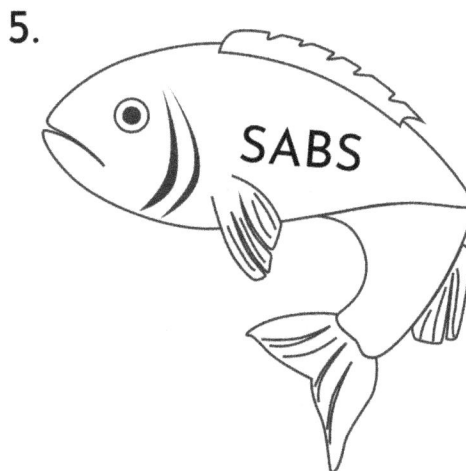

1. _____

2. _____

3. _____

4. _____

5. _____

Word Bank

salmon
sunfish
trout
minnow
sculpin
bass
whitefish
catfish

Amphibians

Two species of toad and two species of frogs live in Canyonlands National Park. Salamanders live there too. Frogs and toads both spend the beginning of their lives the same way - as tadpoles. Tadpoles hatch from eggs, usually in springs or pools of water.

Both frogs and toads are amphibians. Salamanders are amphibians too. Color the amphibians below.

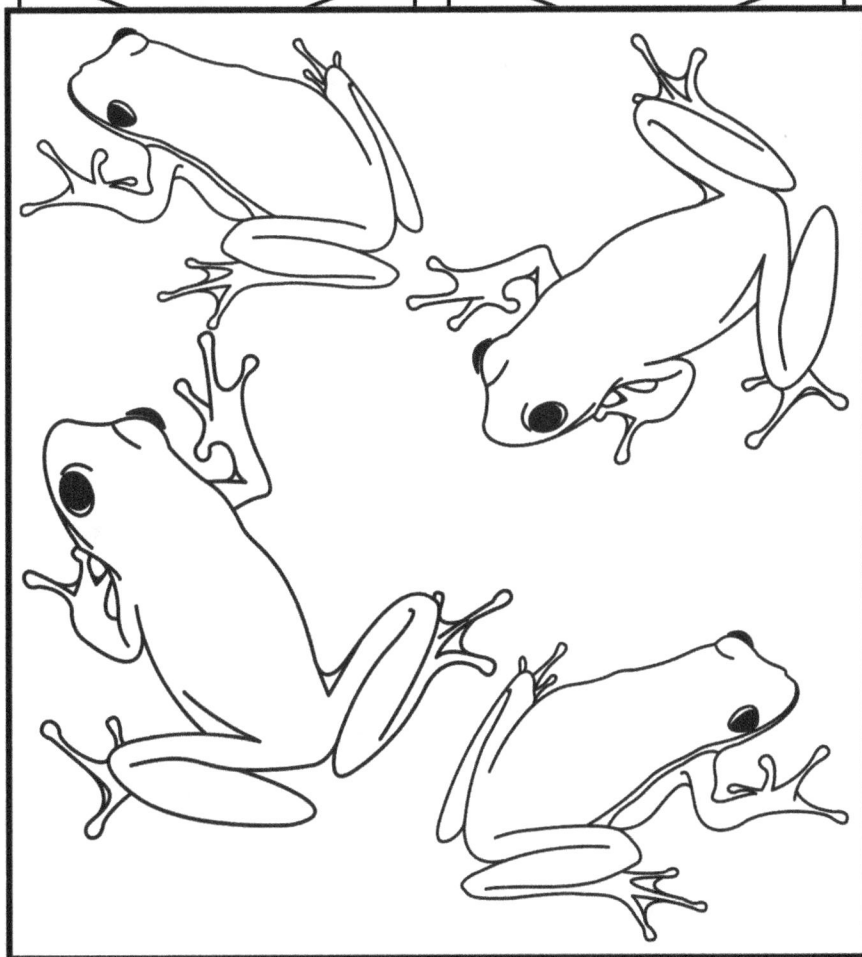

Exploring the Dark Sky

This park is a popular destination for stargazing. You may see stars in the night sky here that you may not see at home. Why do you think that is?

For all of time, people from across the world have looked at the night sky and seen images in the stars. They created stories about groups of stars, also called constellations. Create your own constellation that you see in the starfield below!

What is your constellation named?

Who Lives in Canyonlands?

Below are 9 plants and animals that live in the park. Use the word bank to fill in the clues below. Pay attention to how many letters each word has to see where it fits.

[ ][ ][ ][ ][ ][ ]■ S [ ][ ][ ][ ]

[ ] O [ ][ ][ ]

[ ] U [ ][ ][ ][ ][ ]

[ ][ ][ ] T [ ][ ][ ][ ][ ][ ]

[ ] H [ ][ ][ ][ ][ ][ ]

[ ][ ][ ][ ][ ][ ]■ W [ ][ ][ ]

[ ][ ][ ][ ][ ][ ]■[ ] E [ ][ ]

[ ] S [ ][ ][ ]

[ ][ ][ ][ ] T [ ][ ][ ][ ][ ]

WORD BANK:

CHEATGRASS, GOPHER SNAKE, BOBCAT, CANYON WREN, BULLFROG, PRICKLY PEAR, COTTONTAIL, OSPREY, WHIPTAIL

63 National Parks

How many other national parks have you been to? Which one do you want to visit next? Note that if some of these parks fall on the border of more than one state, you may check it off more than once!

Alaska
- ☐ Denali National Park
- ☐ Gates of the Arctic National Park
- ☐ Glacier Bay National Park
- ☐ Katmai National Park
- ☐ Kenai Fjords National Park
- ☐ Kobuk Valley National Park
- ☐ Lake Clark National Park
- ☐ Wrangell-St. Elias National Park

American Samoa
- ☐ National Park of American Samoa

Arizona
- ☐ Grand Canyon National Park
- ☐ Petrified Forest National Park
- ☐ Saguaro National Park

Arkansas
- ☐ Hot Springs National Park

California
- ☐ Channel Islands National Park
- ☐ Death Valley National Park
- ☐ Joshua Tree National Park
- ☐ Kings Canyon National Park
- ☐ Lassen Volcanic National Park
- ☐ Pinnacles National Park
- ☐ Redwood National Park
- ☐ Sequoia National Park
- ☐ Yosemite National Park

Colorado
- ☐ Black Canyon of the Gunnison National Park
- ☐ Great Sand Dunes National Park
- ☐ Mesa Verde National Park
- ☐ Rocky Mountain National Park

Florida
- ☐ Biscayne National Park
- ☐ Dry Tortugas National Park
- ☐ Everglades National Park

Hawaii
- ☐ Haleakala National Park
- ☐ Hawai'i Volcanoes National Park

Idaho
- ☐ Yellowstone National Park

Kentucky
- ☐ Mammoth Cave National Park

Indiana
- ☐ Indiana Dunes National Park

Maine
- ☐ Acadia National Park

Michigan
- ☐ Isle Royale National Park

Minnesota
- ☐ Voyageurs National Park

Missouri
- ☐ Gateway Arch National Park

Montana
- ☐ Glacier National Park
- ☐ Yellowstone National Park

Nevada
- ☐ Death Valley National Park
- ☐ Great Basin National Park

New Mexico
- ☐ Carlsbad Caverns National Park
- ☐ White Sands National Park

North Dakota
- ☐ Theodore Roosevelt National Park

North Carolina
- ☐ Great Smoky Mountains National Park

Ohio
- ☐ Cuyahoga Valley National Park

Oregon
- ☐ Crater Lake National Park

South Carolina
- ☐ Congaree National Park

South Dakota
- ☐ Badlands National Park
- ☐ Wind Cave National Park

Tennessee
- ☐ Great Smoky Mountains National Park

Texas
- ☐ Big Bend National Park
- ☐ Guadalupe Mountains National Park

Utah
- ☐ Arches National Park
- ☐ Bryce Canyon National Park
- ☐ Canyonlands National Park
- ☐ Capitol Reef National Park
- ☐ Zion National Park

Virgin Islands
- ☐ Virgin Islands National Park

Virginia
- ☐ Shenandoah National Park

Washington
- ☐ Mount Rainier National Park
- ☐ North Cascades National Park
- ☐ Olympic National Park

West Virginia
- ☐ New River Gorge National Park

Wyoming
- ☐ Grand Teton National Park
- ☐ Yellowstone National Park

Other National Parks Crossword

Besides Canyonlands National Park, there are 62 other diverse and beautiful national parks across the United States. Try your hand at this crossword. If you need help, look at the previous page for some hints.

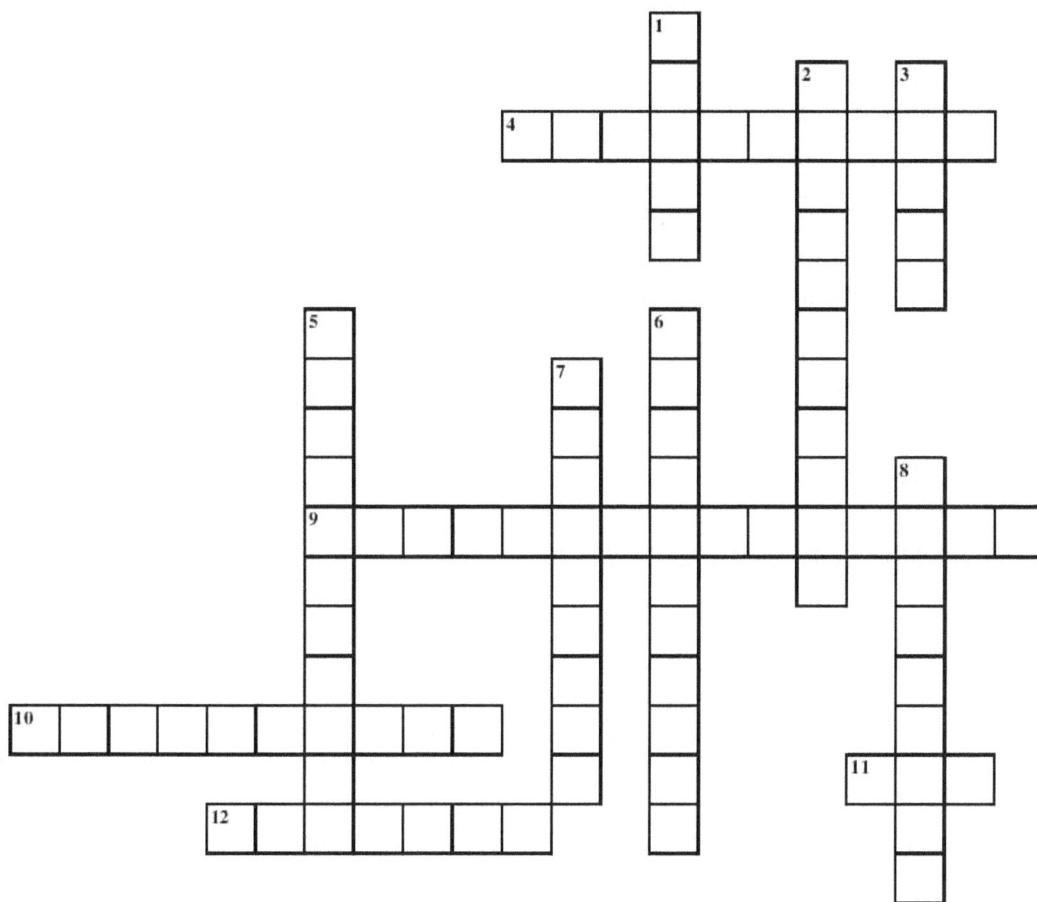

Down

1. State where Acadia National Park is located
2. This national park has the Spanish word for turtle in it
3. Number of national parks in Alaska
5. This national park has some of the hottest temperatures in the world
6. This national park is the only one in Idaho
7. This toothsome creature can famously be found in Everglades National Park
8. Only president with a national park named for them

Across

4. This state has the most national parks.
9. This park has some of the newest land in the US, caused by volcanic eruptions.
10. This park has the deepest lake in the United States.
11. This color shows up in the name of a national park in California.
12. This national park deserves a gold medal.

Which National Park Will You Go to Next? Word Search

1. ZION
2. BIG BEND
3. GLACIER
4. OLYMPIC
5. SEQUOIA
6. BRYCE
7. MESA VERDE
8. BISCAYNE
9. WIND CAVE
10. GREAT BASIN
11. KATMAI
12. YELLOWSTONE
13. VOYAGEURS
14. ARCHES
15. BADLANDS
16. DENALI
17. GLACIER BAY
18. HOT SPRINGS

```
F M M E S A V E R D E B N E Y
E A B I G B E N D E S A S E M
Y L I C A L O Y N E E D L T G
D M G A S S A U C N R L U E R
C E L I I T S C R E O A A K E
S N A W Y E E O I W T N A C A
G I C H A A Q C S E M D N S T
N O I Z P R U T I M R S N E B
I W E L M P O N B W E B K H A
R J R F D N I F L I H B U C S
P A B E E S A N E S O P W R I
S J A E N Y A C S I B A U A N
T C Y I A D O H H Y M E A L R
O T A T L M L E S E G R W R J
H S T O I K A T M A I R O P B
I C H U R C O L Y M P I C O U
O Y G T S D E O S B R Y C E T
W I N D C A V E I N R O H E M
```

52

Field Notes

Spend some time reflecting on your trip to Canyonlands National Park. Your field notes will help you remember the things you experienced. Use the space below to write about your day.

While I was at Canyonlands National Park...

I saw:

_____

_____

_____

_____

I heard:

_____

_____

_____

I felt:

_____

_____

Draw a picture of your favorite thing in the park.

_____

_____

I wondered:

_____

_____

_____

_____

_____

ANSWER KEY

National Park Emblem Answers

1. This represents all plants: **Sequoia Tree**

2. This represents all animals: **Bison**

3. This represents the landscapes: **Mountains**

4. This represents the waters protected by the park service: **Water**

5. This represents the historical and archeological values: Arrowhead

Jumbles Answers

1. PICNICKING

2. HIKING

3. BIRDING

4. CAMPING

5. STARGAZING

6. SIGHTSEEING

7. HORSEBACK RIDING

When Nature Calls...

1. recycling
2. urinate
3. ecosystem
4. flush
5. plumbing
6. pit
7. container
8. flow
9. never
10. ashes
11. hard
12. inches

Answers: National Park Names

ERRIV
(R) I V E R

CETERYME
(C) E M E T E R Y

SHSEAREO
S (E)(A) S H O R E

ESERVER
R (E) S E R V E

ARWAYPK
P A R K W (A) Y

MRIAEMOL
M (E) M O R I A L

RELASHOKE
L A K E S H (O) R E

Now arrange the circled letters to solve one last type of NPS unit.

(R) (E) (C) R (E) (A) T I (O) N   A R (E) (A)

Go Birdwatching at Island in the Sky

start here

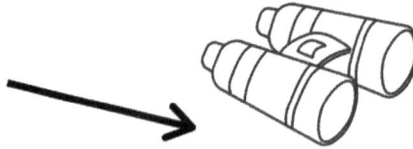

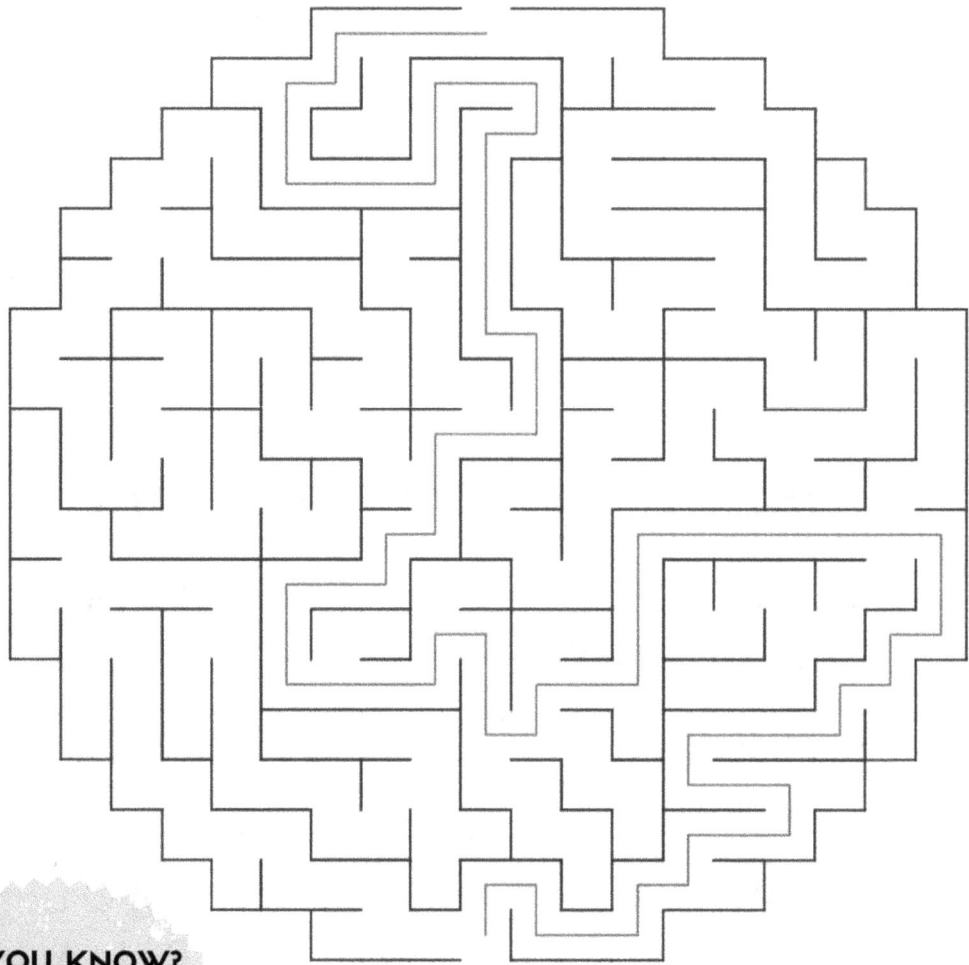

DID YOU KNOW?
Canyonlands NP is home to several birds of prey, including eagles, hawks, and owls. Birds of prey are birds that hunt other animals for food.

Find the Match!
Common Names and Latin Names

Match the common name to the scientific name for each animal. The first one is done for you. Use clues on the page before and after this one to complete the matches.

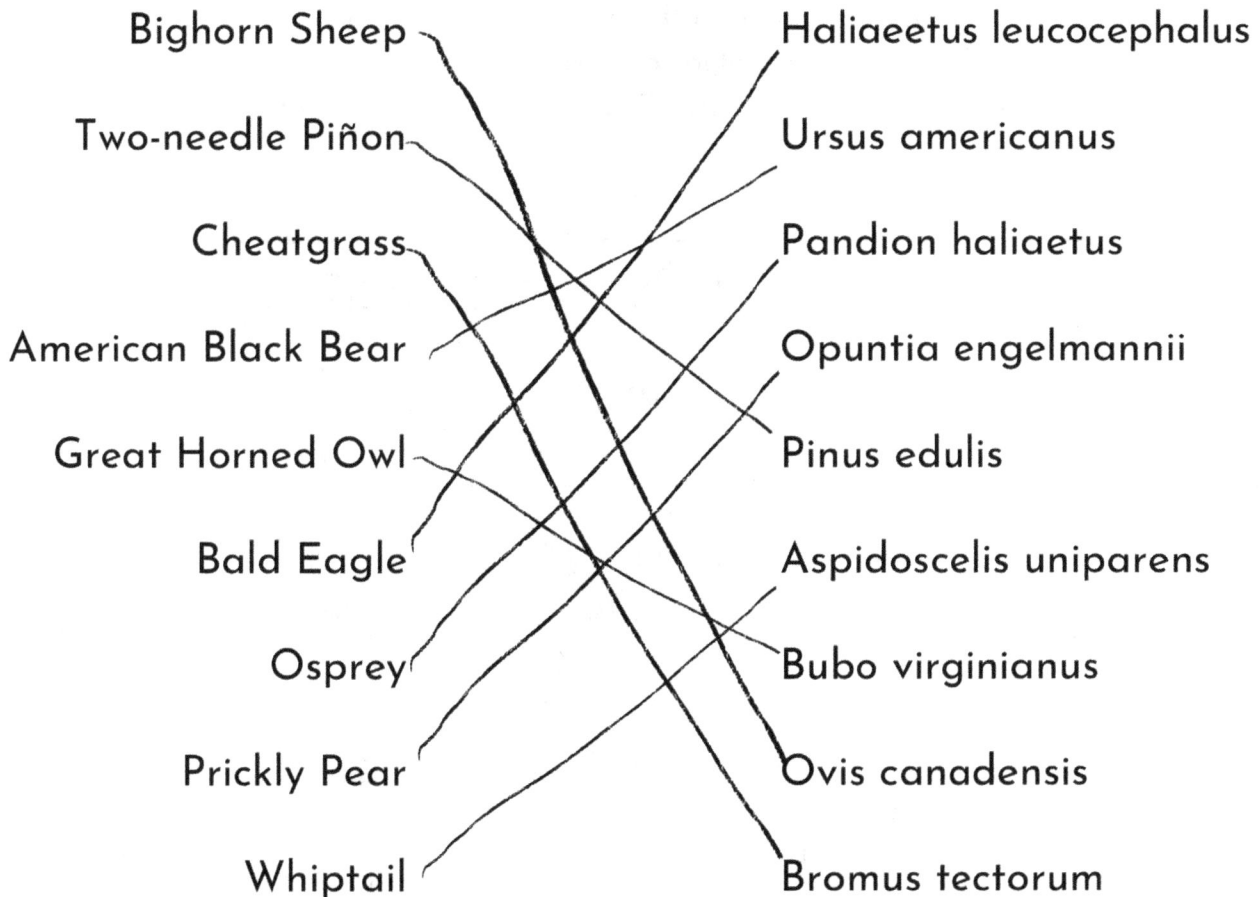

Bighorn Sheep   Haliaeetus leucocephalus

Two-needle Piñon   Ursus americanus

Cheatgrass   Pandion haliaetus

American Black Bear   Opuntia engelmannii

Great Horned Owl   Pinus edulis

Bald Eagle   Aspidoscelis uniparens

Osprey   Bubo virginianus

Prickly Pear   Ovis canadensis

Whiptail   Bromus tectorum

Bald Eagle

Haliaeetus leucocephalus

Answers: The Ten Essentials

The ten essentials are a list of things that are important to have when you go for longer hikes. If you go on a hike to the <u>backcountry</u>, it is especially important that you have everything you need in case of an emergency. If you get lost or something unforeseen happens, it is good to be prepared to survive until help finds you.

The ten essentials list was developed in the 1930s by an outdoors group called the Mountaineers. Over time and technological advancements, this list has evolved. Can you identify all the things on the current list? Circle each of the "essentials" and cross out everything that doesn't make the cut.

(fire: matches, lighter, tinder, and/or stove)	~~a pint of milk~~	~~extra money~~	(headlamp, plus extra batteries)	(extra clothes)
(extra water)	~~a dog~~	~~Polaroid camera~~	~~bug net~~	~~lightweight games, such as a deck of cards~~
(extra food)	~~a roll of duct tape~~	(shelter)	(sun protection such as sunglasses, sun-protective clothes, and sunscreen)	(knife, plus a gear repair kit)
~~a mirror~~	(navigation: map, compass, altimeter, GPS device, or satellite messenger)	(first aid kit)	~~extra flip-flops~~	~~entertainment such as video games or books~~

Backcountry - a remote undeveloped rural area.

Canyonlands Word Search

Words may be horizontal, vertical, diagonal,
or they might be backwards!

1. NEEDLES
2. VULTURES
3. HIGH DESERT
4. SKY
5. MAZE
6. GREEN RIVER
7. MOAB
8. MAZE TRAILS
9. BOATING
10. CAIRN
11. SPIRE
12. MESA
13. WEATHER
14. NARROWLEAF
15. PINYON
16. BIGHORN
17. STARGAZING

```
M O A B G N I M N R I A C D M
E A I E P W A N R A O R U T H
O L Z M A I T H O U R I N G O
S N E E D L E S H Y V R T H A
T D E S Y O T G S N P O G H
A G D A L R G H I I S I N W I
R E G N I T A O B G V A P N G
G L M A R Y O I E U E T I R H
A T N A R R O W L E A F W C D
Z S Y U H E S T T S N A S A E
I G R A F E U D R C A N T M S
N N D H R R R G R K H M A Z E
G I E W E A I O I F T I P I R
D P B S R S N N N A S K Y N T
R M N L E R G D S C P N U G O
W E A T H E R E L E I A M E N
O C R T R A V E R T R N E W D
B O G R E E N R I V E R A D M
```

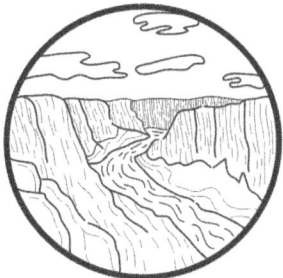

59

Answers: Find the Match!
What are Baby Animals Called?

Match the animal to its baby. The first one is done for you.

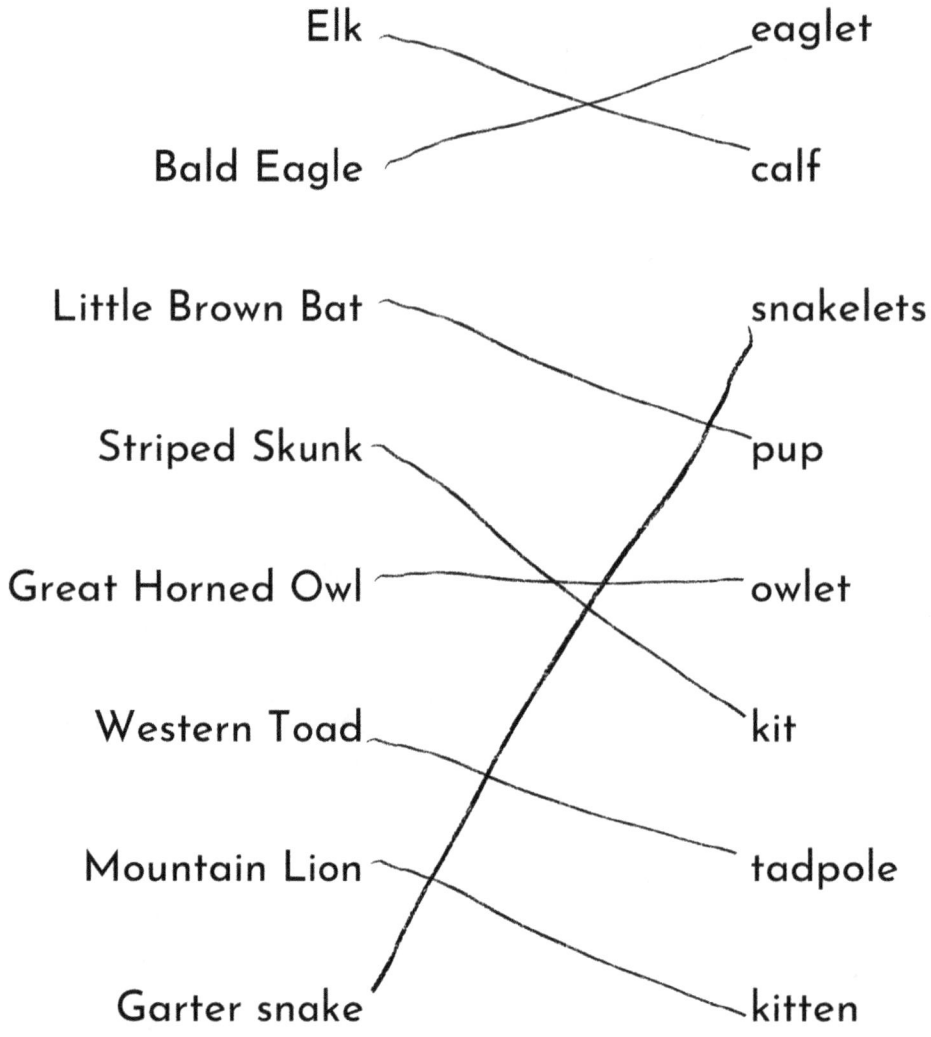

Elk — eaglet

Bald Eagle — calf

Little Brown Bat — snakelets

Striped Skunk — pup

Great Horned Owl — owlet

Western Toad — kit

Mountain Lion — tadpole

Garter snake — kitten

Answer: Hike to a Hoodoo

start
here

DID YOU KNOW?
Hoodoos are tall, thin rocks that protrude from the bottom of a basin. Have you seen any in the park?

Utah Word Search

Words may be horizontal, vertical, diagonal,
or they might be backwards!

1. OSPREY
2. UTAH
3. SOUTHWEST
4. CANYON
5. EXPLORE
6. REPTILE
7. DRY
8. DESERT
9. HIKING
10. ROCKS
11. SALT LAKE CITY
12. GEOLOGY
13. PINYON PINE
14. PINE NUTS
15. CLIFFS
16. BEEHIVE
17. ARID
18. CACTUS

```
C W S O U T H W E S T L O W K
H T A A K I L O C H E L A N J
T G E O L O G Y C C L B A P E
P M P A Y T R S C E R L H L X
I I A D R A L L O E I U I A P
N O N D I R A D C T T K S L
Y E S E E H E K K B P R I C O R
O L B A N U I E G E N E N A R
N E H S G U L O R E C D G D E
P C I C A C T U S H P I O E A
I T A L C H I S O I K E T S N
N R N I K O E I O V O K I Y E
E I O F H Z D E S E R T L G W
J C G F L O V E P O O R V E H
N I L S K H I N R O C K S E A
X T A I A E E G E Z E P R N L
H T D T O E N O Y N A C C I E
U J U O S N E D N Y M A L A Z
```

62

Answers: Leave No Trace Quiz

Leave No Trace is a concept that helps people make decisions during outdoor recreation that protects the environment. There are seven principles that guide us when we spend time outdoors, whether you are in a national park or not. Are you an expert in Leave No Trace? Take this quiz and find out!

1. How can you plan ahead and prepare to ensure you have the best experience you can in the National Park?

    A. Make sure you stop by the ranger station for a map and to ask about current conditions.

2. What is an example of traveling on a durable surface?

    A. Walking only on the designated path.

3. Why should you dispose of waste properly?

    C. So that other peoples' experiences of the park are not impacted by you leaving your waste behind.

4. How can you best follow the concept "leave what you find?"

    B. Take pictures but leave any physical items where they are.

5. What is not a good example of minimizing campfire impacts?

    C. Building a new campfire ring in a location that has a better view.

6. What is a poor example of respecting wildlife?

    A. Building squirrel houses out of rocks from the river so the squirrels have a place to live.

7. How can you show consideration of other visitors?

    B. Wear headphones on the trail if you choose to listen to music.

Solution: Catch a Fish in the Colorado River

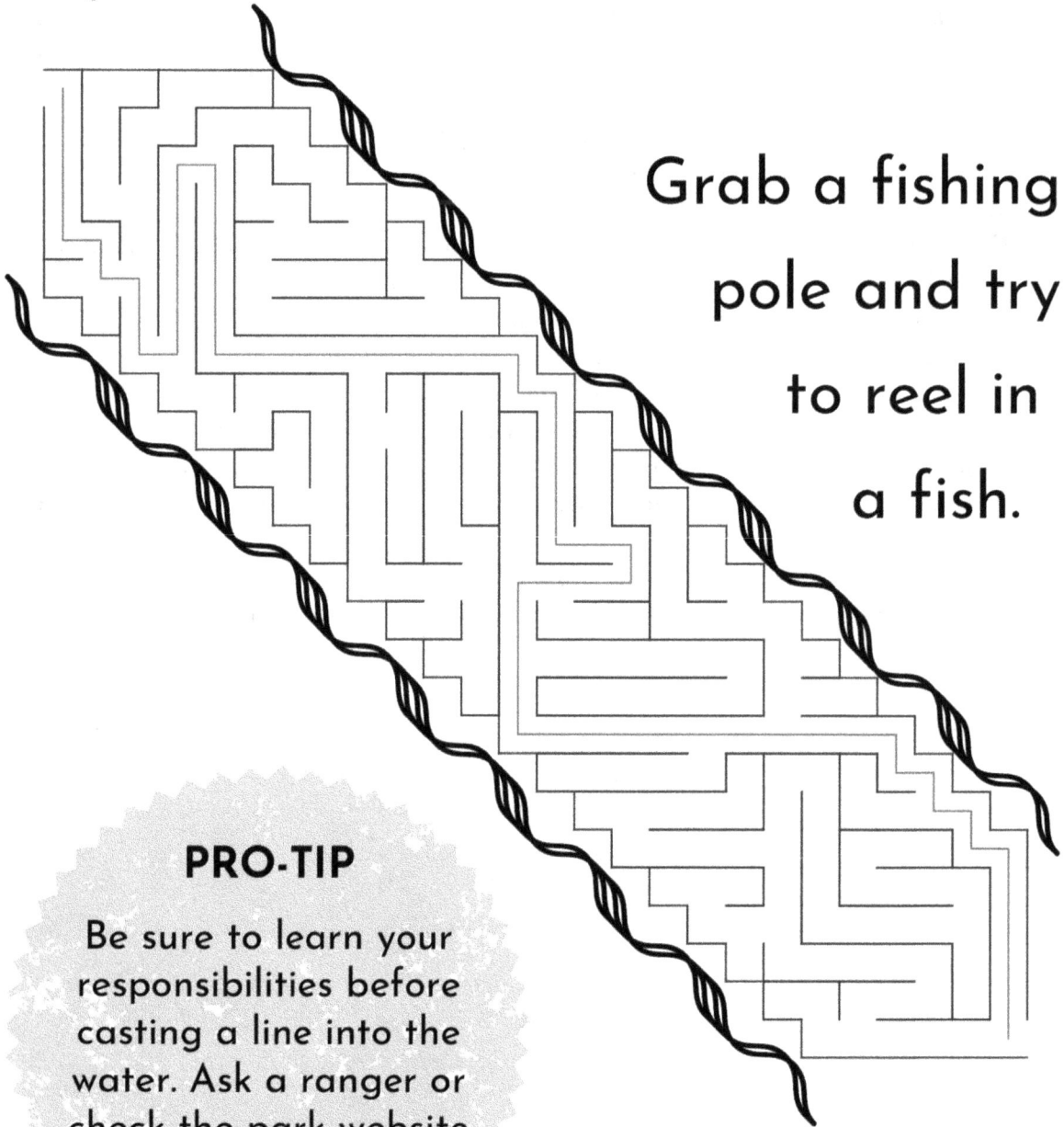

Grab a fishing pole and try to reel in a fish.

PRO-TIP

Be sure to learn your responsibilities before casting a line into the water. Ask a ranger or check the park website before you go.

Decoding Using American Sign Language

American Sign Language, also called ASL for short, is a language that many Deaf people or people who are hard of hearing use to communicate. People use ASL to communicate with their hands. Did you know people from all over the country and world travel to national parks? You may hear people speaking other languages. You might also see people using ASL. Use the American Manual Alphabet chart to decode some national parks facts.

This was the first national park to be established:

Y E L L O W S T O N E

This is the biggest national park in the US:

W R A N G E L L -

S T . E L I A S

This is the most visited national park:

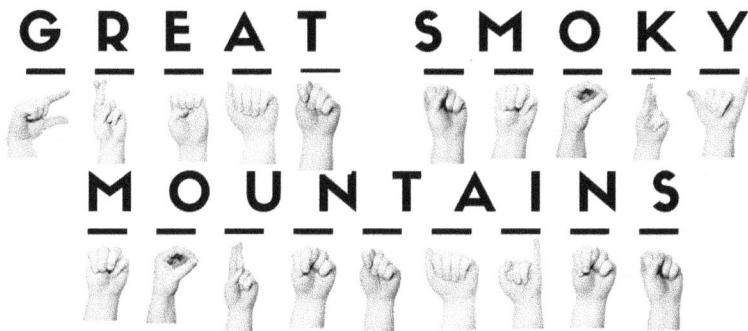

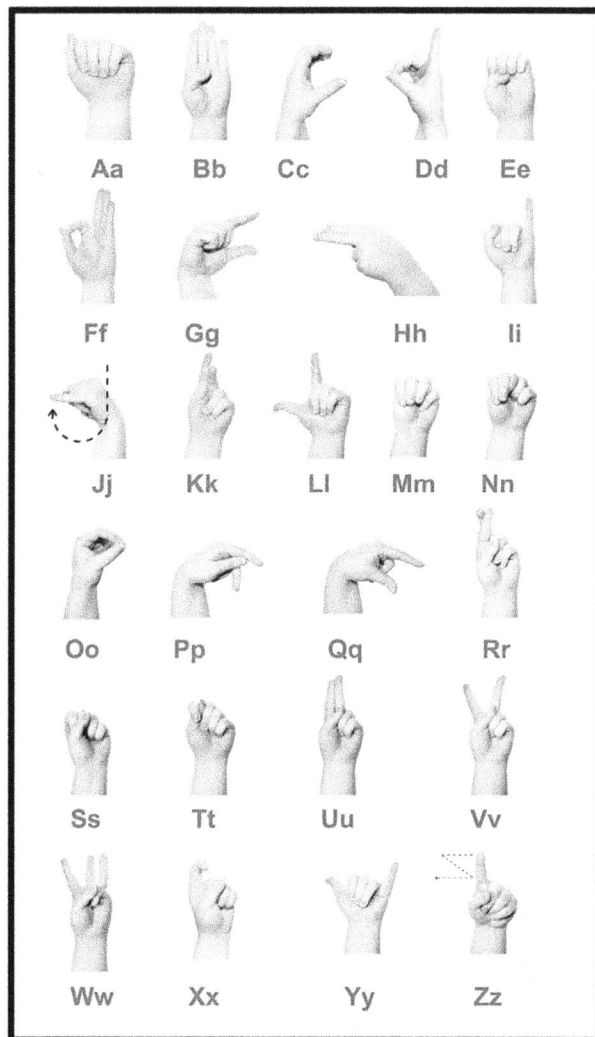

G R E A T   S M O K Y

M O U N T A I N S

Aa	Bb	Cc	Dd	Ee
Ff	Gg		Hh	Ii
Jj	Kk	Ll	Mm	Nn
Oo	Pp	Qq		Rr
Ss	Tt	Uu		Vv
Ww	Xx	Yy	Zz	

Hint: Pay close attention to the position of the thumb!

Try it! Using the chart, try to make the letters of the alphabet with your hand. What is the hardest letter to make? Can you spell out your name? Show a friend or family member and have them watch you spell out the name of the national park you are in.

Go Horseback Riding at Horseshoe Canyon

Help find the horse's lost shoe!

start here →

DID YOU KNOW?

Horseback riding is a popular activity in Canyonlands National Park. There are many trails that you can take horses for day or overnight trips.

Let's Go Camping
Word Search

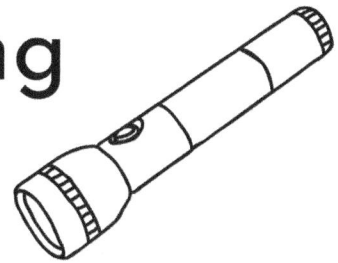

1. TENT
2. CAMP STOVE
3. SLEEPING BAG
4. BUG SPRAY
5. SUNSCREEN
6. MAP
7. FLASHLIGHT
8. PILLOW
9. LANTERN
10. ICE
11. SNACKS
12. SMORES
13. WATER
14. FIRST AID KIT
15. CHAIR
16. CARDS
17. BOOKS
18. GAMES
19. TRAIL
20. HAT

```
D P P I L L O W D B T E A C I
E O A D P R E A A M B R C A N
P W C A M P S T O V E I H X G
R A H S G E L E B E E D A P S
E L B U G S P R A Y N G I E A
S I A H G C I C N N M E R C N
C W N L A F I R S K O O B F K
M T A E M I L E L H M R W L J
T A P R E A O R E S L B A A B
S M P A S R R T E N T L U S C
C E A I I R C G P E I U J H A
S S N A C K S S I M O K I L R
I J R S F O I S N J R A Q I D
C Y E T L E V E G U O R V G S
E W T A K C A B B S S O H H M
X J N F I R S T A I D K I T T
U A A E S S E N G E T P V A B
C J L I A R T D N A M A H A S
```

Fish at Canyonlands National Park

Unscramble the common names of these fish that live in the park.

1.  FITSCAH

2.  OTRTU

3.  LASNOM

4.  SISHFUN

5. 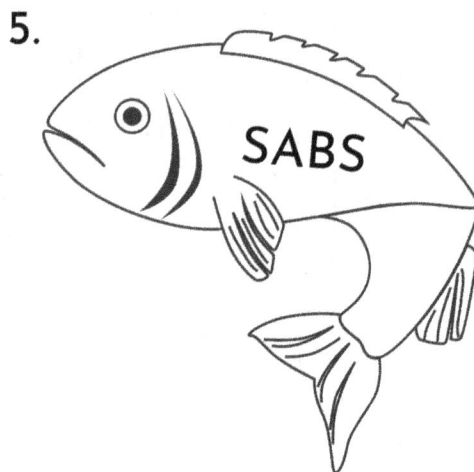 SABS

1. __CATFISH__
2. __TROUT__
3. __SALMON__
4. __SUNFISH__
5. __BASS__

Word Bank

salmon
sunfish
trout
minnow
sculpin
bass
whitefish
catfish

Answers: Who Lives in Canyonlands?

Below are 9 plants and animals that live in the park. Use the word bank to fill in the clues below. Pay attention to how many letters each word has to see where it fits.

GOPHER ■ S NAKE

B O BCAT

B U LLFROG

COT T ONTAIL

W H IPTAIL

CANYON ■ W REN

PRICKLY ■ P E AR

O S PREY

CHEA T GRASS

WORD BANK:

CHEATGRASS, GOPHER SNAKE, BOBCAT, CANYON WREN, BULLFROG, PRICKLY PEAR, COTTONTAIL, OSPREY, WHIPTAIL

Answers: Other National Parks

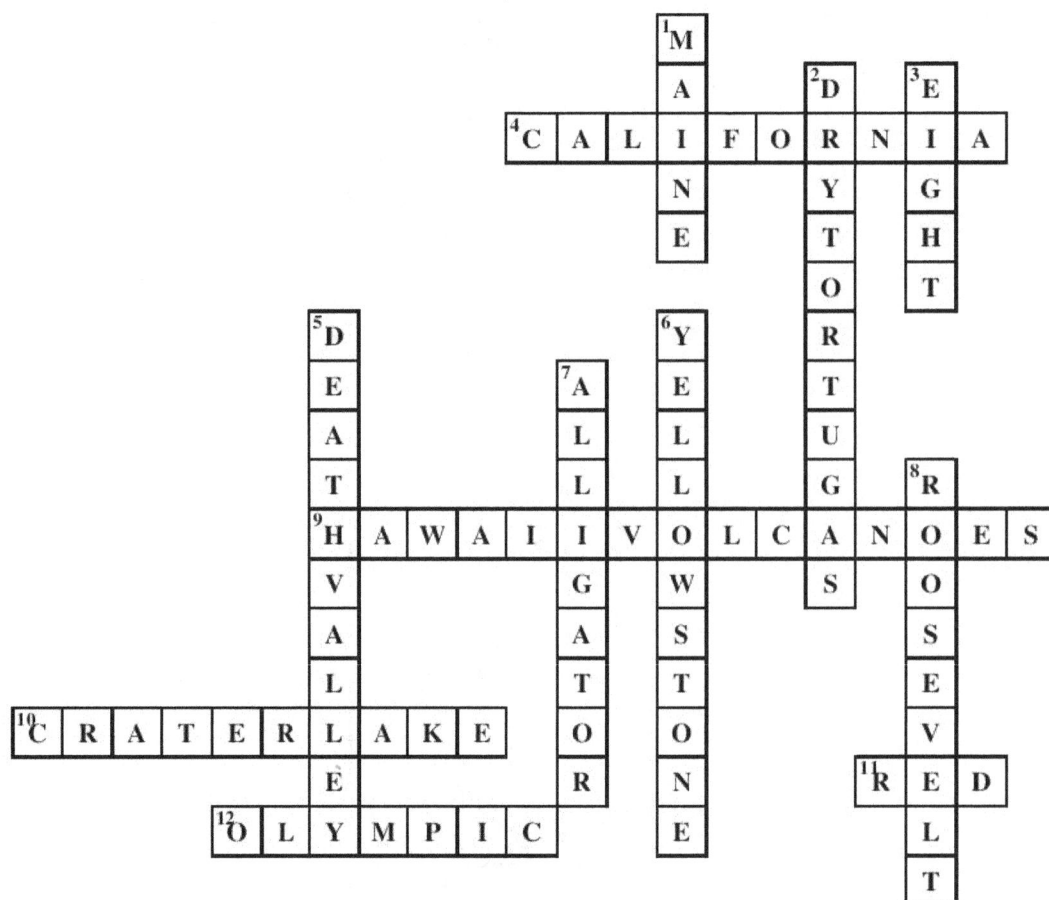

Down

1. State where Acadia National Park is located
2. This National Park has the Spanish word for turtle in it
3. Number of National Parks in Alaska
5. This National Park has some of the hottest temperatures in the world
6. This National Park is the only one in Idaho
7. This toothsome creature can famously be found in Everglades National Park
8. Only president with a national park named for them

Across

4. This state has the most National Parks
9. This park has some of the newest land in the US, caused by a volcanic eruption
10. This park has the deepest lake in the United States
11. This color shows up in the name of a National Park in California
12. This National Park deserves a gold medal

Answers: Which National Park Will You Go To Next?

1. ZION
2. BIG BEND
3. GLACIER
4. OLYMPIC
5. SEQUOIA
6. BRYCE
7. MESA VERDE
8. BISCAYNE
9. WIND CAVE
10. GREAT BASIN
11. KATMAI
12. YELLOWSTONE
13. VOYAGEURS
14. ARCHES
15. BADLANDS
16. DENALI
17. GLACIER BAY
18. HOT SPRINGS

```
F  M  M  E  S  A  V  E  R  D  E  B  N  E  Y
E  A  B  I  G  B  E  N  D  E  S  A  S  E  M
Y  L  I  C  A  L  O  Y  N  E  E  D  L  T  G
D  M  G  A  S  S  A  U  C  N  R  L  U  E  R
C  E  L  I  I  T  S  C  R  E  O  A  A  K  E
S  N  A  W  Y  E  E  O  I  W  T  N  A  C  A
G  I  C  H  A  A  Q  C  S  E  M  D  N  S  T
N  O  I  Z  P  R  U  T  I  M  R  S  N  E  B
I  W  E  L  M  P  O  N  B  W  E  B  K  H  A
R  J  R  F  D  N  I  F  L  I  H  B  U  C  S
P  A  B  E  E  S  A  N  E  S  O  P  W  R  I
S  J  A  E  N  Y  A  C  S  I  B  A  U  A  N
T  C  Y  I  A  D  O  H  H  Y  M  E  A  L  R
O  T  A  T  L  M  L  E  S  E  G  R  W  R  J
H  S  T  O  I  K  A  T  M  A  I  R  O  P  B
I  C  H  U  R  C  O  L  Y  M  P  I  C  O  U
O  Y  G  T  S  D  E  O  S  B  R  Y  C  E  T
W  I  N  D  C  A  V  E  I  N  R  O  H  E  M
```

LITTLE BISON
Press

Little Bison Press is an independent children's book publisher based in the Pacific Northwest. We promote exploration, conservation, and adventure through our books. Established in 2021, our passion for outside spaces and travel inspired the creation of Little Bison Press.

We seek to publish books that support children in learning about and caring for the natural places in our world.

To learn more, visit:
www.littlebisonpress.com

Want more free games and activities? Visit our website!